CHILDREN'S ENCYCLOPEDIA OF MATHS

Tim Collins

Picture Credits:

Every attempt has been made to clear copyright. Should there be any inadvertent omission, please apply to the publisher for rectification.

Key: b-bottom, t-top, c-centre, l-left, r-right

Alamy: 18-19 (Vintage Images), 80br (The Granger Collection), 88cl (Pictorial Press Ltd), 93tr (Everett Collection Historical), 102-103 (NASA Archive), 106-107 (Petro Feketa), 119br (Science History Images); **Bridgeman Library**: 92br (Prismatic Pictures); **Getty Images**: 4-5 (alenkadr), 28br (Grafissimo), 48-49 (JoeChristensen), 58-59 (AfricaImages), 68-69 (monkeybusinessimages), 86-87 (DragonImages), 90-91 (Asia-Pacific Images Studio); **NASA Images**: 102br (David C Bowman/ NASA); **Science Photo Library**: 52-53 (William Putman / Nasa Goddard Space Flight Center / Science Photo Library), 85br (Emilio Segre Visual Archives / American Institute of Physics / Science Photo Library); **Shutterstock**: 1 (Butterfly Hunter), 4bl (ping198), 5t (Zzzufa), 5c (Christian Mueller), 5br (Kwadrat), 6-7 (Petr Kratochvila), 6-7c (Chanrit spp), 6b (dachnarong wangkeeree), 7tr (rawf8), 7br (AGCuesta), 8-9 (Suwan Wanawattanawong), 9tr (SumanBhaumik), 10-11 (Krasula), 10cl (zoff), 10b (Oliver Denker), 11tr (jason cox), 12-13 (Krakenimages.com), 12b (zentilia), 13tr (lenetstan), 13br (Jason Winter), 14-15 (Bulltus_casso), 15br (cloki), 17cr (LarsZ), 17b (luchschenF), 18bl (Zakharchuk), 19br (Shaynedrinkstockphoto), 20-21 (Mark Brandon), 21cr (Marina Keremkhanova), 22-23 (Tobik), 22bl (Lesya Dolyuk), 23br (Chekyravaa), 24-25 (Anatoli Styf), 24b (MehmetO), 25t (rasoulali), 25br (Fabio Balbi), 26-27 (brizmaker), 26b (Stefania Valvola), 28-29 (Nick Brundle), 28c (Lorelyn Medina), 30-31 (matimix), 30c (N.Vinoth Narasingam), 31tr (elfinadesign), 32-33 (Blackregis), 32c (pics721), 33tr (Pan Media), 33br (Patrick Foto), 34-35 (Achkin), 34bl (kmls), 35tr (Grigorita Ko), 35b (FabrikaSimf), 36-37 (Liudmyla Chuhunova), 37tr (A.Sych), 38-39 (Damsea), 39tr (LStockStudio), 39br (santon1982), 40-41 (miroslavmisiura), 41t (Peter Hermes Furian), 41bl (MNI), 42-43 (Brent Hofacker, 42bl (Fractal Channel), 43cr (local_doctor), 44-45 (Poring Studio), 44cl (RomanMr), 44br (Piotr Wawrzyniuk), 45cr (aaltair), 46-47 (Vincenzofoto), 46b (Allvidmix), 47tr (luckyraccoon), 47br (Julenochek), 48c (Stray Toki), 49tr (elnavegante), 50-51 (Ekaterina Pokrovsky), 50c (Shaun Jeffers), 50br (Ron Kolet), 51bl (G.Tbov), 52br (Prachaya Roekdeethaweesab), 53bl (Maridav), 53br (PRILL), 54-55 (MAGNIFIER), 54bl (Rostislav_Sedlacek), 55c (Castleski), 56-57 (Andrey Burmakin), 56b (Thirteen), 57tr (Arinchawit Jit), 57bl (Nikolay Antonov), 58bl (Olemac), 59tl (mikesj11), 59br (1000 Words), 60-61 (Skycolors), 60br (Stu Porter), 61t (melhijad), 61br (Eric Gevaert), 62-63 (Triff), 62b (Meister Photos), 63c (Denis Belitsky), 63br (Nixx Photography), 64-65 (Maria Savenko), 65br (Invisible Studio), 66-67 (IR Stone), 66br (spacezerocom), 67tl (Akhenaton Images), 68br (Denis Belitsky), 69br (qingqing), 70-71 (mooremedia), 71t (Liya Graphics), 71br (Holiday.Photo.Top), 72-73 (Southtownboy Studio), 72bl (SOMKKU), 73tr (adriano77), 73bl (Abby Dude), 74-75 (dade72), 74bl (Mari-Leaf), 75tr (HandmadePictures), 76-77 (David Herraez Calzada), 76br (Everett Collection), 77tr (Line By Line Vectors), 77cr (VectorsMarket), 78-79 (Maren Winter), 78bl (Borka Kiss), 79br (Vladimir Shulenin), 80-81 (Gearstd), 81br (Studio KIWI), 82-83 (irin-k), 82bl (kievstock), 83tr (Eddie J. Rodriquez), 83b (Muanpare Wanpen), 84-85 (AlphaBoom), 84bl (Vadim Sadovski), 85tr (Evelyn D. Harrison), 86br (photo by jaja), 87c (21MARCH), 87b (Photogrape), 88-89 (Elena Schweitzer), 89tr (Graeme Dawes), 89cr (Claudio Divizia), 90c (panda_o), 90br (EKKAPHAN CHIMPALEE), 91bl (PaO_STUDIO), 94-95 (Maksim Shmeljov), 94bl (Brian A Jackson), 95c (Meankw), 95br (Rawpixel.com), 96-97 (Karasev Victor), 96br (Dmitry Kalinovsky), 97t (neopicture), 97bl (Danila Shtantsov), 98-99 (Pascal Guay), 98bl (Bertl123), 99tr (Dan Breckwoldt), 99br (Marco Rubino), 100-101 (Monkey Business Images), 100c (Olena Yakobchuk), 102c (Dotted Yeti), 104-105 (Anton Gvozdikov), 105tr (Robert Kneschke), 105br (German Vizulis), 106bl (Shiler), 107tr (Everett Collection), 107b (DeawSS), 108-109 (Dean Drobot), 109tr (tarczas), 109c (SpeedKingz), 109br (Brttny Smth), 110c (Andrey_Popov), 110-111 (ID1974), 111t (Feng Yu), 112bl (BestPhotoPlus), 114-115 (Rasica), 114b (Everett Collection), 115tr (chelovector), 116-117 (Andrii Vodolazhskyi), 116b (M-SUR), 118-119 (Szasz-Fabian Jozsef), 119t (Sunbunny Studio), 120-121 (elRoce), 120br (Vereshchagin Dmitry), 121tr (tomtsya), 121c (S.Myshkovsky), 122-123 (Jamie Roach), 122bl (Max4e Photo), 123cr (Boris Medvedev), 123br (Mr.Somchai Sukkasem), 124-125 (Phonlamai Photo), 124br (vkilikov), 125br (Pan Media); **Wikimedia Commons**: 9br (Prathu134), 19tr (Agence de presse Mondial Photo-Presse) 40br (Adolf Neumann, Digitaler Portrait Index), 43br (Rama), 55tr (Godfrey Kneller), 64br (Frans Hals), 88br (Illustrated London News), 92-93 (Antoine Taveneaux), 93bl (Hubert Berberich), 103tr (NASA on The Commons), 115br (Hans Peters), 117tr (Justinc). **Cover images** all from Shutterstock. Front: (Doug Lemke), front tl (Oko Laa), front tcl (Christos Georghiou), tc (Min C. Chiu), tcr (arslaan), tr (GreenArt), back (Anatoli Styf), front flap (TigerStocks), back flap (SOMKKU).

This edition published in 2021 by Arcturus Publishing Limited
26/27 Bickels Yard, 151–153 Bermondsey Street,
London SE1 3HA

Copyright © Arcturus Holdings Limited

All rights reserved. No part of this publication may be reproduced, stored in a retrieval system, or transmitted, in any form or by any means, electronic, mechanical, photocopying, recording or otherwise, without prior written permission in accordance with the provisions of the Copyright Act 1956 (as amended). Any person or persons who do any unauthorised act in relation to this publication may be liable to criminal prosecution and civil claims for damages.

ISBN: 978-1-78950-458-3
CH007213UK
Supplier 29, Date 1120, Print run 10280

Printed in China

Author: Tim Collins
Designer: Lorraine Inglis
Picture Research: Lorraine Inglis and Paul Futcher
Consultant: Anne Rooney
Editor: Becca Clunes
Art Director: Jessica Holliland
Managing Editor: Joe Haris

CHILDREN'S ENCYCLOPEDIA OF MATHS

CONTENTS

Introduction	4

CHAPTER ONE: NUMBERS

Counting	6
Zero	8
Negative Numbers	10
Base 10	12
Powers	14
Large Numbers	16
Infinity	18
Prime Numbers	20
Fractions	22
Algebra	24

CHAPTER TWO: GEOMETRY

Triangles	26
Angles	28
Polygons	30
3-D Shapes	32
Scaling Up	34
Pi	36
Symmetry	38
Topology	40
Fractals	42
Patterns in Nature	44

CHAPTER THREE: MEASUREMENTS

Distance	46
Time	48
Dates	50
Temperature	52
Weight	54
SI Units	56
Money	58
Motion	60
Light Years	62
Maps	64

CHAPTER FOUR: STATISTICS AND PROBABILITY

Data	66
Averages	68
Correlation	70
Frequency	72
Graphs	74
Charts	76
Growth	78
Probability	80
Estimation	82
Chaos Theory	84

CHAPTER FIVE: TECHNOLOGY

The Abacus	86
The Computer	88
Barcodes	90
Secret Codes	92
Security	94
Traffic	96
Buildings	98
Algorithms	100
Space Travel	102
Networks	104

CHAPTER SIX: MATHS IN LIFE

Puzzles	106
Music	108
Searching	110
Game Theory	112
Art	114
Diseases	116
Sequences	118
Weather	120
Sport	122
Logic	124

GLOSSARY	126
INDEX	128

Introduction

Maths has been with us ever since early humans began to count days and objects, and assigned the first words and symbols to numbers. It's played a vital role in the development of civilization, as we progressed from hunter-gatherers to settled farmers to our sophisticated modern lives.

Maths is Everywhere

Maths shapes our world whether we realise it or not. Without it, we wouldn't have phones and computers, we wouldn't be able to fly around the world, and we would never have gone into space. We owe much in our modern lives to the great pioneers of maths.

An abacus is a counting tool used for carrying out mathematical operations. It was the forerunner of the calculator and is still used today in some countries.

A googolplex contains more zeros than you could write, even if you spent the rest of your life trying.

Numbers

Maths is about numbers. From the ten digits you can count on your fingers and thumbs to the huge sequences of zeros and ones used by your devices. As you discover maths, you'll be introduced to things like negative numbers, the mysterious primes, and numbers so big you could never write them down.

Shapes

Geometry is the branch of maths that deals with shapes. It fascinated the ancient Egyptians and Greeks, and still affects us today. It can help us make stronger buildings and more precise maps, and even paint better pictures.

This "geodesic dome" uses triangles to form a rigid structure.

Data

Gathering data and looking for patterns in it is more important than ever. Data is used to track all aspects of our lives and make predictions about everything from the weather to the spread of diseases.

Data has been called one of the most valuable resources in the modern world. Details about our lives and habits are sought after by big companies.

Measurements

Anything can be measured, from the distance between your house and your school, to the time it takes you to get there. Maths helps us create standard units so we can compare our measurements with others.

Lots of old measurements were based on body parts. Some survive today, as when the height of a horse is measured in "hands."

DID YOU KNOW? Some people work out maths problems in their head using a "mental abacus." They imagine an abacus is in front of them and mime moving the beads around.

Chapter 1: Numbers

Counting

Early humans counted by making marks on sticks and cave walls. It helped them keep track of days, animals, and people. These marks are known as "tallies" and they're still sometimes used as a simple counting method.

The First Numbers

As humans settled and began to farm, counting became even more important. They needed to trade with others, and tally marks developed into the first systems of numbers. Simple operations like addition, subtraction, division, and multiplication were soon established.

This is the most famous method of tallying, but it's not the only one. Another system uses dots joined by straight lines.

A straight line is used to stand for each day, person, or object.

At first, only straight lines were used, but this made large numbers hard to manage.

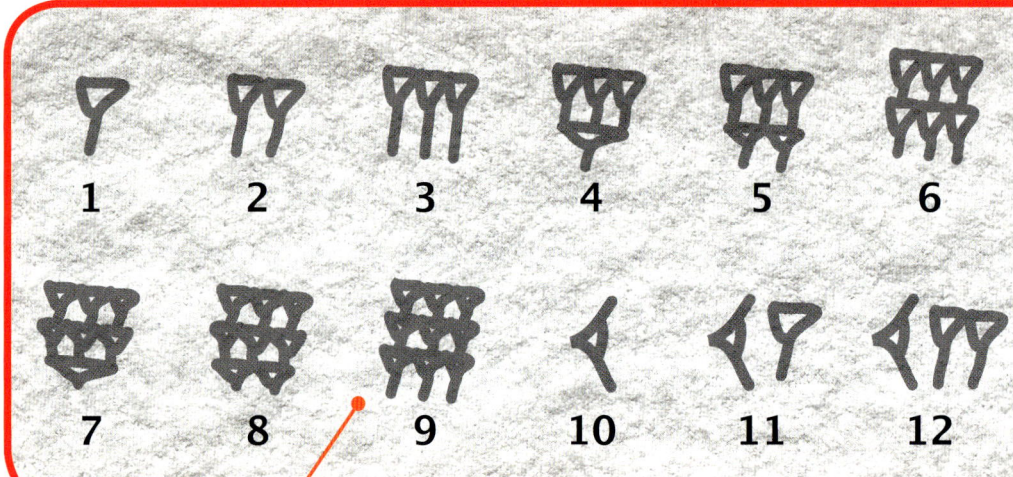

Cuneiform was the writing system of the Ancient Sumerians, who lived in the area now known as Iraq. They used symbols to represent numbers, making wedge-shaped marks on a clay tablet with a stylus.

MATHS FACT: The Four Operations

The four basic mathematical operations are addition, subtraction, multiplication, and division.

Addition: 2 + 2 = 4
Subtraction: 8 − 6 = 2
Multiplication: 3 × 3 = 9
Division: 10 ÷ 2 = 5

A diagonal stroke was added to group marks into five and make them easier to read.

Roman Numerals

The Ancient Romans used letters to stand for numbers:

I = 1   X = 10   C = 100   M = 1000
V = 5   L = 50   D = 500

You can build other numbers from these by placing them alongside each other. When a small number appears after a bigger one, it means you add it. When a small number appears before a bigger one, it means you subtract it. For example, XI means 10 plus 1, which is 11. And IX means 10 minus 1, which is 9.

Roman numerals are still used today on clocks, on the outside of buildings, and in the titles of movies and games.

DID YOU KNOW? The digits from 0 to 9 that we use today are known as "Hindu-Arabic numerals." This is because they were developed in India and North Africa before coming to Europe.

Zero

It might seem obvious that zero comes before one, but it actually took a long time for nothing to become a number. Early counting systems such as Roman numerals didn't include zero. It was only with the work of Brahmagupta in the 7th century that zero established its place in maths.

Place Value Systems

Zero is very helpful in place value systems, where the value of a digit is determined by its position. For example, when we see the number 348, we know it's made up of three 100s, four 10s, and eight 1s. Without zero, it would be difficult to tell the difference between numbers like 21, 201, and 2,010.

> An ancient Indian text discovered in the 19th century was found to use a large dot to stand for zero. This is thought to have developed into the zero symbol we use today.

Empty Spaces

Merchants in ancient China kept track of what they'd bought and sold by putting rods on a counting board. They used a place value system, where the position of the rods on the board reveals their value. They used an empty space to stand for zero.

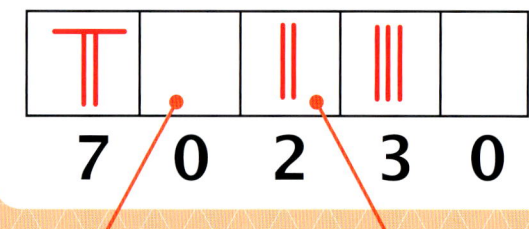

An empty space is used for zero. It works on a counting grid, but becomes confusing when the numbers are written down. A clear symbol was needed to stand for zero.

These rods stand for the numbers 7, 2, and 3. They create the number 70,230 because of their positions on the board.

DID YOU KNOW? The Ancient Maya number system used a drawing of a shell to represent zero. The other numbers were made from dots and lines.

0:00 is used on digital stopwatches, and on 24-hour clocks, where it stands for midnight.

Without zero as a placeholder, we couldn't differentiate between times like one minute and one second, and one minute and ten seconds.

Zero is vital for money. It would be hard to know if someone was giving you £1, £10, or £100 without it.

Dividing by zero is impossible. If you imagine dividing 12 sweets between three friends, they would get four each. But if you imagine dividing them by zero friends, the example stops making sense.

HALL OF FAME: Brahmagupta

Brahmagupta, shown here in a rather idealized portrait, was an Indian mathematician who lived in the 7th century. He was the first person to treat zero as a number in its own right rather than just a placeholder. He came up with rules for calculating with zero, some of which are still used today.

9

Negative Numbers

Negative numbers can seem quite abstract. It's easy to imagine what three cookies look like, but what do minus three look like? Despite this, we are often faced with negative numbers in real life. We can find them everywhere from thermometers to elevator panels.

On an elevator panel, the floors below ground level are shown as negative numbers.

Negative and Positive

Lots of early civilizations had ways to record debt, so in a sense they used negative numbers. But negative numbers were only brought into the same number system as positive ones by the Indian mathematician Bramagupta in the 7th century. He stated that a positive number subtracted from zero becomes a negative one.

Zero on the Celsius scale is the freezing point of water.

MATHS FACT: Sea Level

Negative numbers are used to describe places below sea level. The deepest known spot in any ocean is the Mariana Trench in the Pacific, which has an elevation of −10,994 metres. If you could place Mount Everest in the trench, its peak would still not reach the surface of the water.

10

Temperatures can be measured on both the Celsius and the Fahrenheit scale. Zero degrees Fahrenheit is a lot colder than zero degrees Celsius.

In the Red

In ancient China, black counting rods were used for money owed and red ones were used for money received. On modern bank statements, the colours are the other way around, with debt shown in red. That's why people in debt are sometimes called "in the red."

Negative numbers are used to show debt. The amount owed to the bank is printed in red and preceded by a minus symbol.

Scientists use a third scale, known as the "Kelvin scale." This starts at "absolute zero," the lowest temperature possible, and features no negative numbers.

A temperature of below zero is one of the ways we encounter negative numbers in daily life.

DID YOU KNOW? Multiplying a negative number by a positive number gives a negative number. But multiplying a negative number by another negative number gives a positive number.

Base 10

The counting and number system we use every day is "base 10," also known as decimal. It features ten digits, which are 0, 1, 2, 3, 4, 5, 6, 7, 8, and 9. If you want to count higher than 9, you have to add an extra digit to create 10. The "1" stands for the number of times you've used up all the digits and had to start again.

Humans have ten fingers and thumbs, which explains why the base 10 number system has been the most popular throughout history.

Other Number Systems

Base 10 might seem natural to us, but there are many other number systems. Some people think we should use base 12, or "duodecimal" instead, because the number 12 can be divided by 2, 3, 4, and 6, whereas 10 can only be divided by 5 and 2. They think this makes the system easier to use. But it would be very hard to make people change something they've used their whole lives.

If humans had just three fingers and a thumb on each hand, the base 8 system would probably be the most common.

Binary

Computers use the base 2 system, which is known as "binary." Instead of ten digits, it features just "0" and "1." It suits computers because they use electrical signals that are either off or on. 0 stands for off, and 1 stands for on.

Movies, songs, maps, and anything else is stored as data in huge sequences of 0s and 1s on your computer, phone, or tablet.

Ever found it strange that the time goes straight from 11:59 to 12:00? It's because clocks use a base 60 system for seconds and minutes.

The same numbers are written differently in each system. 10 in decimal is 1010 in binary.

Not every culture uses base 10. The Arara people of Brazil have developed a base 2 system.

MATHS FACT: Number Systems

Binary (base 2) uses two digits: 0, 1

Octal (base 8) uses eight digits: 0, 1, 2, 3, 4, 5, 6, 7

Hexadecimal (base 16) uses ten digits and six characters: 0, 1, 2, 3, 4, 5, 6, 7, 8, 9, A, B, C, D, E, F

DID YOU KNOW? France tried to enforce decimal time in the 1790s. Each day was split into ten hours, each hour was split into a hundred minutes, and each minute was split into a hundred seconds.

13

Powers

If you multiply a whole number by itself, you get a square number. For example, $3 \times 3 = 9$. If you multiply a whole number by itself and then by itself again, you get a cube number. For example, $3 \times 3 \times 3 = 27$. These calculations can be written as 3^2 and 3^3 respectively. In this notation, the large digit is known as the "base" and the small digit is known as the "power."

> The Rubik's cube is a popular puzzle based on a $3 \times 3 \times 3$ cube. It gives the impression of being made of 27 smaller cubes, though the middle piece is actually cross-shaped.

High Powers

The base and the power can be changed to any number. For example, 4^5 means "four to the power of 5" or $4 \times 4 \times 4 \times 4 \times 4 = 1,024$. Powers can help us to deal with very large numbers. For example, a trillion can be written as 10^{12}, which is easier to take in than 1,000,000,000,000.

The square root of 25 is 5, because 5 multiplied it by itself is 25.

Square Roots

The opposite of squaring a number is called finding the "square root." The square root of a number can be multiplied by itself to give the original number. The symbol √ is used in mathematical notation, so we might write $\sqrt{25} = 5$.

> There are over 43 quintillion combinations of a Rubik's cube. This huge number can be written as 43 followed by 18 zeroes.

DID YOU KNOW? A square number can only end with the digits 0, 1, 4, 5, 6, or 9.

MATHS FACT: Changing the Power

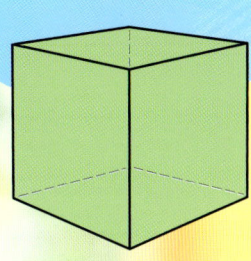

Base and Power	Written as	Expanded	Value
2^2	Two squared	2×2	4
2^3	Two cubed	$2 \times 2 \times 2$	8
2^4	Two to the power of four	$2 \times 2 \times 2 \times 2$	16
2^5	Two to the power of five	$2 \times 2 \times 2 \times 2 \times 2$	32

Each face of a Rubik's cube is 3 squares long and 3 squares high, making a total of 9 squares. This can be written as 3^2.

The mass of the Earth in scientific notation is 5.97×10^{24} kg.

Scientists use powers of 10 to write very large numbers. This is known as "scientific notation." For example, the number 7,000,000 would be written as 7×10^6. The power tells you how many zeros you'd have to use if you wrote the entire number out.

15

Large Numbers

Early number systems were used to keep track of time and for trading things like cattle and sheep, so really big numbers weren't needed. But as civilizations developed, larger numbers were required. These days, advances in science mean that huge numbers are used to express things like the amount of cells in the human body, which is estimated at 3.72×10^{13}.

Small Numbers

Very large numbers like the one above need to be written in scientific notation, as they would be too hard to read if written in full. But the same is also true of very small numbers. In these cases, the power of 10 is written as a negative number. For example, the diameter of an atom is around 0.00000001cm, which is written as 1×10^{-8}cm.

> Astronomers deal with distances so vast they measure them in light years. A light year is the distance light travels in a year, which is 9.46×10^{12}km.

> The number of atoms in the observable universe has been estimated as 10^{82}. To write that, you'd have to start with a 1 and add 82 zeros.

MATHS FACT: Names of Large Numbers

A million 10^6	A billion 10^9
A trillion 10^{12}	A quadrillion 10^{15}
A quintillion 10^{18}	A sextillion 10^{21}
A googol 10^{100}	A googolplex 10^{googol}

The number of stars in the observable universe has been estimated as between 10^{22} and 10^{24}.

Expanding Storage

The first hard disk drive was released in 1956 and could store up to 5 megabytes, which is around 5 million bytes of data. By the 1990s, personal computers typically came with a 1 gigabyte drive, around a billion bytes of data. Modern hard drives can hold as much as 10 terabytes, or 10 trillion bytes.

The diameter of our galaxy the Milky Way has been estimated as 9.5×10^{17} km or 100,000 light years.

Technology brings huge numbers into our daily lives. The word "terabyte," meaning "a trillion bytes," entered everyday language as the capacity of hard drives grew.

There are around 5×10^{21} atoms in a single drop of water. This number can also be written as 5 sextillion or 5 followed by 21 zeros.

DID YOU KNOW? It would be impossible to print out all the zeros in a googolplex in a book, as the mass of the book would have to be greater than the mass of the observable Universe.

17

Infinity

Things that come to an end are known as "finite." Things that never come to an end are called "infinite." We know that numbers are infinite, as you can always add one to any number to make it bigger. However, that does not mean infinity itself is a number. It's an idea, and one which has some brain-boggling consequences for maths.

> The mathematician Émile Borel came up with a famous statement about infinity in 1913. He said that a monkey using a typewriter for an infinite amount of time would eventually type any given text, such as the complete works of Shakespeare.

Countable and Uncountable

The German mathematician Georg Cantor (1845–1918) came up with the surprising idea that not all infinities are the same. He stated that some infinite sets are "countable." For example, there are an infinite amount of whole numbers starting 1, 2, 3, 4, 5… but you can begin to count them. But other infinite sets are "non-countable." For example, you can't begin to count all the decimals between 0 and 1. There are an infinite number of them, and an infinite number between 0 and 0.01, 0 and 0.001, and so on.

An Infinite Universe?

Astronomers talk about the "observable universe," but they don't know what exists beyond it. Is it possible that the Universe is infinite? If so, the consequences are mind-melting. If there are an infinite number of planets, there could be an infinite number just like Earth. And on those infinite Earths, there could be an infinite number of people exactly the same as you.

The Universe is vast, but does it eventually end or does it go on forever? Scientists don't know the answer.

HALL OF FAME: Émile Borel (1871–1956)

French mathematician Émile Borel carried out influential work in several areas of maths, such as probability. He is most famous for his idea about a monkey typing all of the books in the French national library. It was intended to show something incredibly unlikely that cannot be mathematically proven to be impossible, but the example took on a life of its own and entered popular culture.

In 2011, an American computer programmer created "virtual monkeys" which were programs generating random characters, to see if they could produce the works of Shakespeare. The monkeys managed it, but only in small blocks of characters that were checked off against the full text.

The monkey example (or ape, as shown here) demonstrates the principle that given an infinite amount of time, an infinite number of events will occur.

A bizarre study in 2003 attempted to bring Borel's idea to life by giving some actual monkeys a computer. They typed five pages, mostly consisting of the letter "s."

Infinity has its own mathematical symbol, which resembles an 8 turned on its side, and is called a "lemniscate." The symbol was given its meaning in the 17th century by the mathematician John Wallis.

DID YOU KNOW? The word "infinity" comes from the Latin word "infinitas" which means "boundless" or "endless."

19

Prime Numbers

Most numbers can be divided into smaller whole numbers. For example, 8 can be divided by 4 and by 2. But some numbers can only be divided by themselves and 1. These are the prime numbers, and they have intrigued us for centuries.

Maths Mysteries

Prime numbers fascinate mathematicians because they're so mysterious. They're simple to understand, but there's no regular pattern to them. Mathematicians are still searching for new primes today, and competing to find the longest. The current record-holder is over 24 million digits long.

The Sieve of Eratosthenes

Eratosthenes was a Greek mathematician born around 276 BCE. He came up with a simple method for finding prime numbers known as a "sieve." You start by listing numbers in a grid and crossing out 1. You go through the numbers, leaving the primes unmarked but crossing out all the multiple of primes.

Two is a prime number, so you leave it and cross out all its multiples.

Three is a prime number, so you leave it and cross out all its multiples.

Four is not a prime number. It has already been crossed out because it's a multiple of 2.

PRIME NUMBERS
2 3 5 7 11 13 17 19 23
29 31 37 41 43 47 53 59
61 67 71 73 79 83 89 97

An insect called the periodical cicada emerges from the underground to lay eggs and breed every 13 or 17 years. Both of these are prime numbers.

20

Living on a prime number schedule, the cicadas avoid predators. Some of their predators have greater populations every two years, and some every three years, so the cicadas avoid them.

Prime numbers have some surprising uses in everyday life. For example, they're used to keep your personal details safe online. A large number created by multiplying two primes together is used as a "lock" and the primes are the "key." Even with a sophisticated computer, it is incredibly difficult to work out which prime numbers multiply together to make a huge number.

If the cicadas emerged every 12 years instead, they would encounter more predators with two, three, and four-year life-cycles.

MATHS FACT: Large Primes

Every few years, someone breaks the record for the longest prime number using software that can be downloaded for free. Could you be the next record-breaker?

Prime Number	Length in Digits	Year Discovered
$2^{82589933} - 1$	24,862,048	2018
$2^{77232917} - 1$	23,249,425	2017
$2^{74207281} - 1$	22,338,618	2016
$2^{57885161} - 1$	17,425,170	2013

DID YOU KNOW? 2 is the only even prime number. The rest are all odd numbers.

Fractions

Fractions tell you how many parts of a whole you have. This can be parts of a whole number, or a whole object, such as a pizza. If you're sharing a pizza with three friends, you might slice it into two halves, and then slice it again into four quarters. Whether you realize it or not, you're using fractions.

Numerator and Denominator

A half can be written as $\frac{1}{2}$. A third can be written as $\frac{1}{3}$. And a quarter can be written as $\frac{1}{4}$. The number on the bottom is called the "denominator," and it shows how many parts the whole has been divided into. The number on the top is called the "numerator" and it shows how many of those parts you have.

You can also express parts of a whole in decimals. Each slice of this cake is $\frac{1}{10}$, which can also be written as 0.1. To convert a fraction into a decimal, simply divide the numerator by the denominator. For example, 1 divided by 10 is 0.1

This pizza has been cut into eight slices. Each slice is $\frac{1}{8}$ of the pizza. In this case, the denominator is 8 and the numerator is 1.

$\frac{1}{8}$ is a "proper" fraction because the numerator is smaller than the denominator.

22

If you had four slices of the pizza, you would have ⁴⁄₈, which is the same as ²⁄₄, which is the same as ½. Writing a fraction in its simplest form like this is known as "reducing" it.

If you took all this pizza and a slice from another one cut the same way, you'd have ⁹⁄₈. This is an "improper" fraction because the numerator is bigger than the denominator.

Percentages

Percentages can express the part of a whole too. Imagine if a cake was cut into 100 slices. If you wanted half of it, you would take 50 slices, or 50%. If you wanted a fifth of it, you'd take 20 slices, or 20%

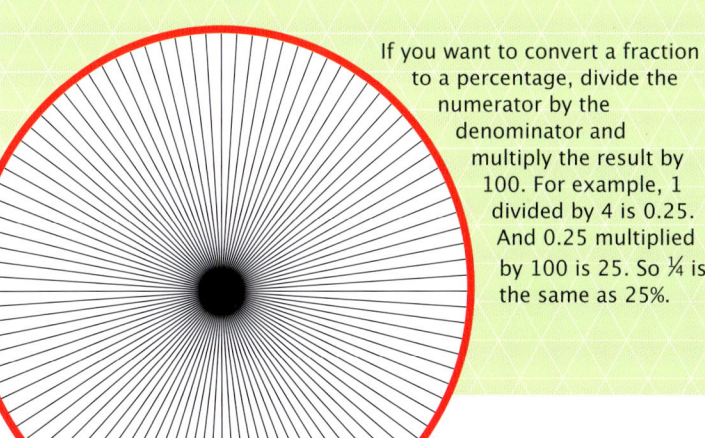

If you want to convert a fraction to a percentage, divide the numerator by the denominator and multiply the result by 100. For example, 1 divided by 4 is 0.25. And 0.25 multiplied by 100 is 25. So ¼ is the same as 25%.

MATHS FACT: Fractions, Decimals, and Percentages

Fraction	Term	Decimal	Percentage
½	A half	0.5	50%
⅓	A third	0.333333	33.333333%
¼	A quarter	0.25	25%
⅕	A fifth	0.2	20%
¹⁄₁₀₀	A hundredth	0.01	1%

DID YOU KNOW? A whole number followed by a fraction is known as a "mixed number." For example, 5½ and 2¾ are mixed numbers.

Algebra

Algebra uses equations to let us calculate quantities we don't know when we have some of the information already. For example, if we know that x + 1 = 2, we can tell that x = 1. The letter x stands for the thing we don't know yet. We could use an empty box or a blank space instead, but using a letter makes it easier to write.

Beyond Maths

Algebra might seem like an abstract part of maths, but it's used in lots of things that affect our lives. It's used in computer science, architecture, geology, accounting, and engineering, among many other fields. It's even used by doctors when they're working out the dosage of medicine to give a sick person.

An equation can be seen as a set of scales. Each side must balance the other.

x + 3

For these scales to balance, the value of x must be 2. Imagine taking 3 away from both sides. You'd be left with x on one side, and 2 on the other. So x = 2.

The letters at the end of the alphabet, x, y, and z, are used for unknown quantities.

HALL OF FAME:
Al-Khwarizmi
(c780 – c850)

Muhammad Ibn Musa al-Khwarizmi was born in what is now Uzbekistan, and moved to Baghdad, where he studied at the House of Wisdom. He is known as the "father of algebra" for establishing the rules for solving equations in his work *The Compendious Book on Calculation by Completion and Balancing.* He also made important contributions to the fields of geography and astronomy.

The Beginnings of Algebra

Algebra can be traced back as far as the ancient Babylonians. It developed from the need to solve practical problems, often to do with farming. But it was in 9th century Baghdad that many of the important principles of algebra were laid down. The term "algebra" comes from the Arabic word "al-jabr," which means "reunion of broken parts."

"The golden age of Islam," which dated from the 8th to the 14th century, saw great advances in several areas of maths, including algebra. Brilliant scholars gathered at the "House of Wisdom" in Baghdad.

Most equations mathematicians deal with are much more complicated than this, but they still work to the same principle of balance.

Some of the most important ideas in science can be written as simple equations. Albert Einstein's famous "$E = mc^2$" means "energy equals mass times the speed of light squared." It was part of Einstein's theory of special relativity, which introduced a new framework for physics.

DID YOU KNOW? The convention of expressing unknown quantities in algebra with x, y, and z was invented by the French mathematician and philosopher René Descartes.

Chapter 2: Geometry

Triangles

Triangles are two-dimensional shapes with three straight sides and three interior angles. They're so fascinating to mathematicians that there's an entire branch of maths called "trigonometry" devoted to them. The term comes from "trigonon," the Greek word for triangle.

Triangles are sturdy shapes that are often used in construction, as seen in this timber roof frame.

Strong Shapes

As well as being incredibly simple, triangles are also very strong. This is why they're used in the design of things like cranes, bridges, and electricity pylons. Some of the most famous modern buildings, such as the Transamerica Pyramid in San Francisco, make use of triangles.

Triangles are grouped into three main kinds—equilateral, isosceles, and scalene. These names tell us how many sides and angles are equal.

An **equilateral triangle** has three equal sides and three equal angles.

An **isosceles triangle** has two equal sides and two equal angles.

A **scalene triangle** has no equal sides and no equal angles.

HALL OF FAME: Pythagoras

Pythagoras was a mathematician and philosopher who lived in ancient Greece from around 570 BCE to 495 BCE. He might not have been the first to come up with the rule about right-angled triangles which is named after him, but he made many important early contributions to maths. He thought everything could be explained with numbers, and founded a community dedicated to studying them.

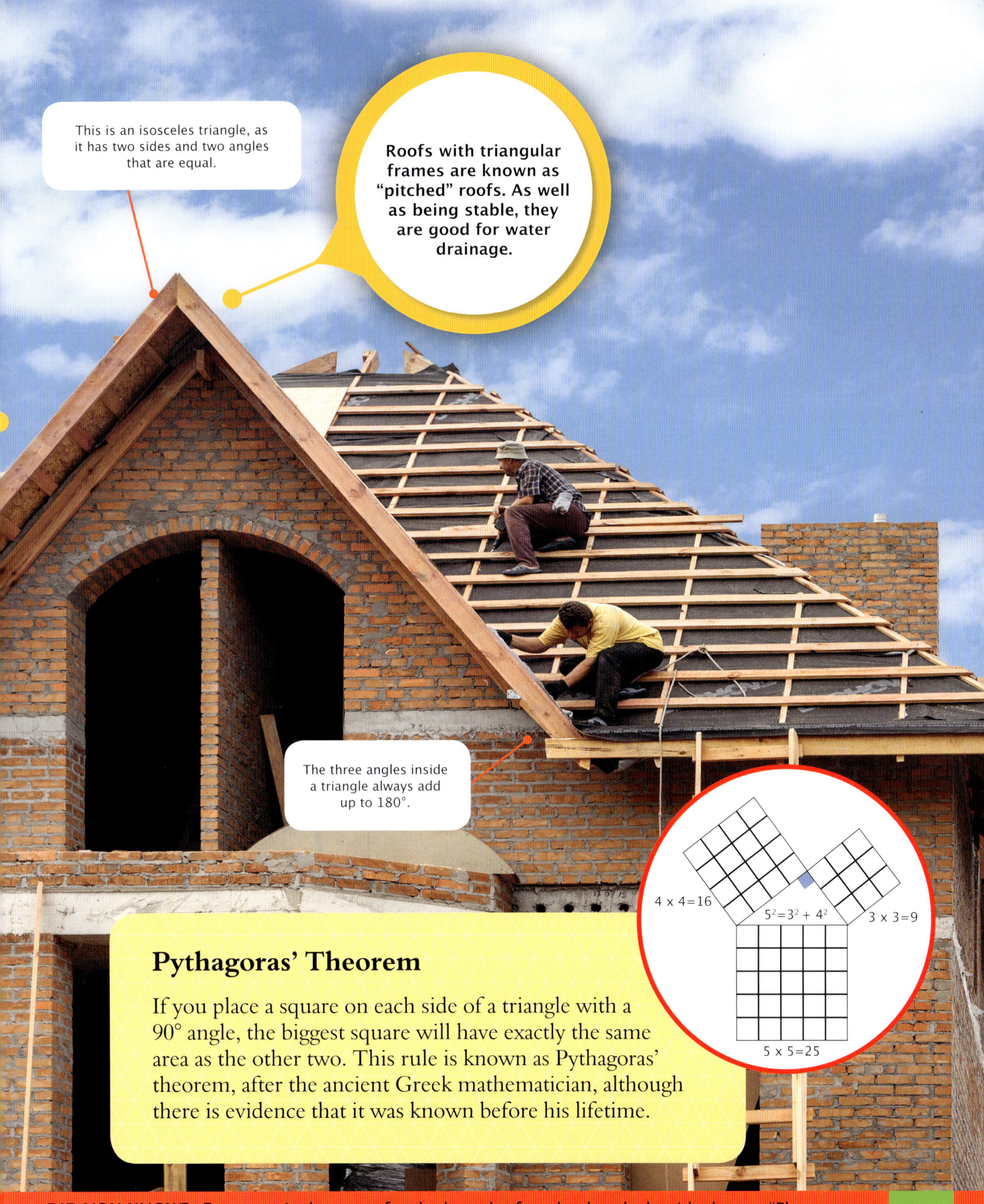

This is an isosceles triangle, as it has two sides and two angles that are equal.

Roofs with triangular frames are known as "pitched" roofs. As well as being stable, they are good for water drainage.

The three angles inside a triangle always add up to 180°.

$4 \times 4 = 16$

$5^2 = 3^2 + 4^2$

$3 \times 3 = 9$

$5 \times 5 = 25$

Pythagoras' Theorem

If you place a square on each side of a triangle with a 90° angle, the biggest square will have exactly the same area as the other two. This rule is known as Pythagoras' theorem, after the ancient Greek mathematician, although there is evidence that it was known before his lifetime.

DID YOU KNOW? Geometry is the name for the branch of maths that deals with shapes. "Plane geometry" is about flat shapes like lines, circles, and triangles.

Angles

Angles are formed when two lines meet at a shared point. They are measured in degrees, which are shown by the symbol °, and tell you the amount of turn between the lines. A half rotation is 180° and a full rotation is 360°.

The Great Pyramid at Giza is the only one of the seven wonders of the ancient world that's still standing, which shows how strong this shape can be.

Angles in Life

Architects and engineers need to measure angles when they're designing things like bridges and houses. Sportspeople calculate angles when they're kicking footballs and throwing basketballs. And whenever you glance at a clock, you're using the angles of the hands to work out the time.

Right angles are exactly 90°. Angles that are less than this are called "acute angles." Angles that are more than 90° but less than 180° are called "obtuse angles." And angles that are more than 180° and less than 360° are called "reflex angles."

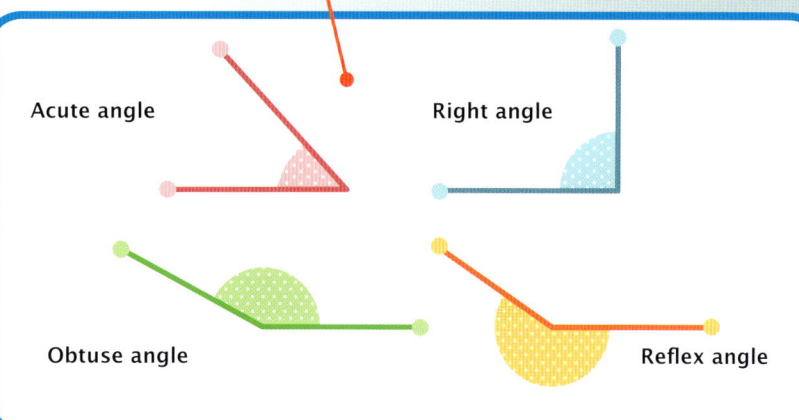

Acute angle | Right angle
Obtuse angle | Reflex angle

HALL OF FAME: Euclid

Euclid was an ancient Greek mathematician who is known as the "father of geometry" for his pioneering ideas about shapes. He gathered them in a work called *Elements* around 300 BCE. It's been called the most influential mathematical work ever written, and remained the standard textbook on geometry for over 2,000 years.

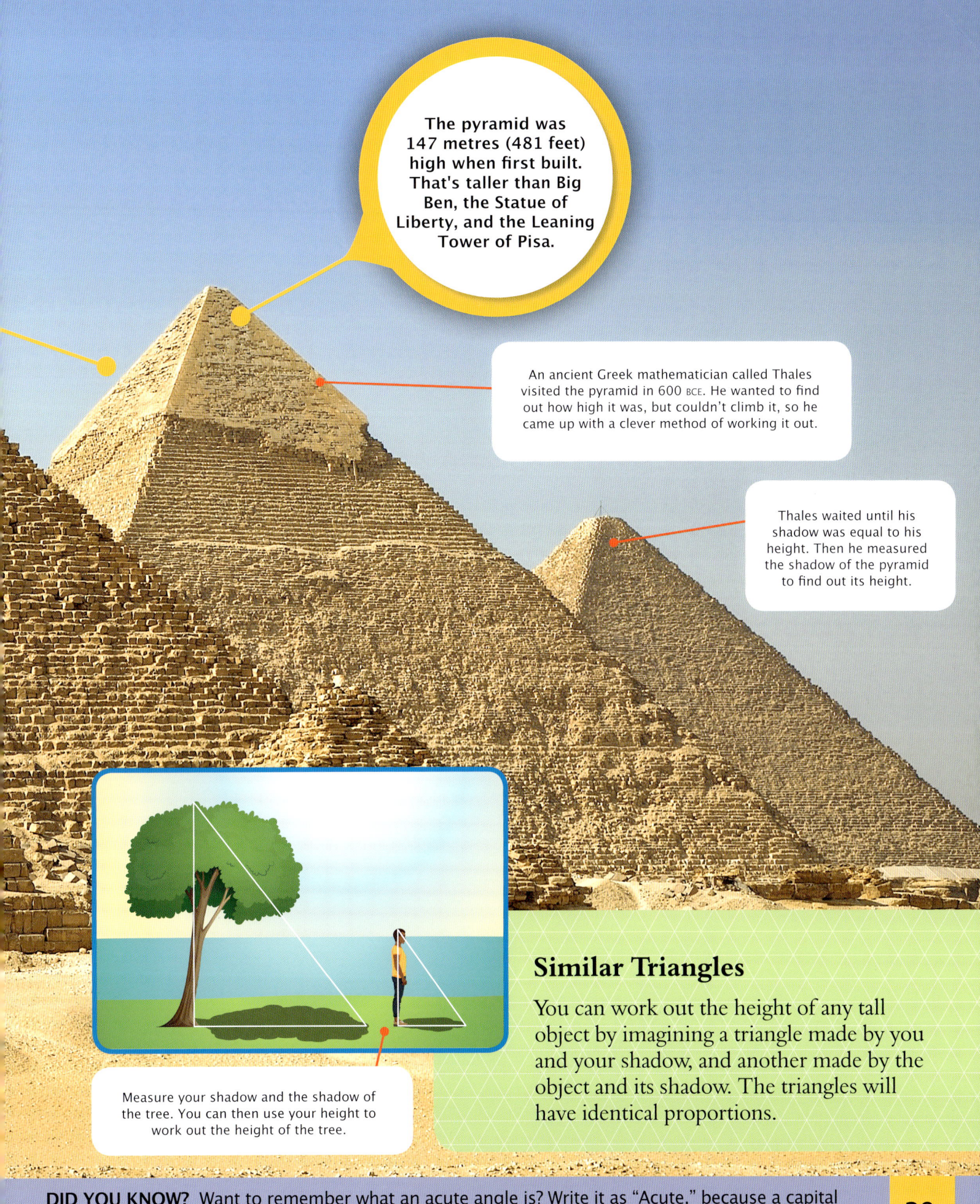

The pyramid was 147 metres (481 feet) high when first built. That's taller than Big Ben, the Statue of Liberty, and the Leaning Tower of Pisa.

An ancient Greek mathematician called Thales visited the pyramid in 600 BCE. He wanted to find out how high it was, but couldn't climb it, so he came up with a clever method of working it out.

Thales waited until his shadow was equal to his height. Then he measured the shadow of the pyramid to find out its height.

Similar Triangles

You can work out the height of any tall object by imagining a triangle made by you and your shadow, and another made by the object and its shadow. The triangles will have identical proportions.

Measure your shadow and the shadow of the tree. You can then use your height to work out the height of the tree.

DID YOU KNOW? Want to remember what an acute angle is? Write it as "Acute," because a capital A looks like an acute angle.

29

Polygons

Polygons are shapes made from straight sides, such as squares, rather than shapes with curves, such as circles. If all the sides and angles of a polygon are equal, it's called a "regular polygon." If they're not, it's called an "irregular polygon."

Quadrilaterals

A regular polygon with four sides is a square. But there are many other well-known polygons with four sides, such as rectangles, rhombuses, parallelograms, and kites. These shapes are known as "quadrilaterals," and their interior angles add up to 360°.

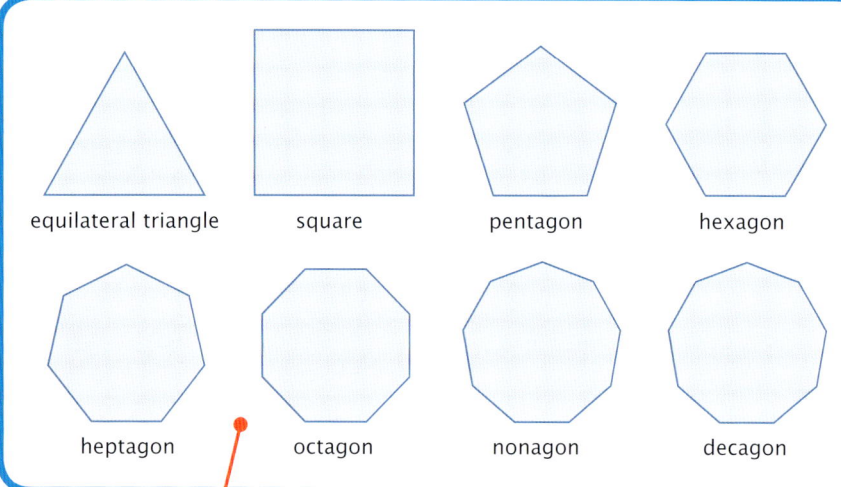

equilateral triangle — square — pentagon — hexagon
heptagon — octagon — nonagon — decagon

The first two regular polygons are the equilateral triangle and the square. After that, the names end in "-gon," which comes from the Greek word for "angle."

The pattern on this football is made up of twelve regular pentagons and twenty regular hexagons.

Regular pentagons have five equal sides and five interior angles of 108°. The sum of the angles is 540°.

MATHS FACT: Regular Polygons

Name	Number of Sides	Interior Angle
Equilateral Triangle	3	60°
Square	4	90°
Pentagon	5	108°
Hexagon	6	120°
Heptagon	7	128.6°
Octagon	8	135°

Tessellation

Some shapes fit together perfectly into a repeating pattern. This is called "tessellation." Only three regular polygons can fit together into a "regular tessellation." These are equilateral triangles, squares, and hexagons. But there are many "semi-regular" tessellations, which combine two or more regular polygons.

Hexagons can be placed into a repeating pattern. They have interior angles of 120°, so three can fit exactly into 360°.

Some road signs use a football symbol made entirely of hexagons. This is possible on a flat surface, but not on a ball. In the UK, a petition was launched to make the signs geometrically accurate.

Regular hexagons have six equal sides and six interior angles of 120°. The sum of the angles is 720°.

DID YOU KNOW? A "chiliagon" is the name for a polygon with 1,000 sides. It looks pretty much the same as a circle, but if you magnify it enough, you can see the straight lines that make it up.

31

3-D Shapes

Mathematicians aren't just interested in 2-D shapes. They are also interested in cubes, spheres, cylinders, and other 3-D ones. The study of 3-D shapes is called "solid geometry," while "plane geometry" deals with 2-D ones.

Polyhedrons

The most important division in 3-D shapes is between polyhedrons and non-polyhedrons. Shapes such as cubes and pyramids are polyhedrons because all their surfaces are flat. Shapes such as spheres and cones are non-polyhedrons because they have curved surfaces.

If a pool has a depth of 2 metres, a width of 3 metres, and a length of 8 metres, then the volume is 2 x 3 x 8 = 48 cubic metres.

Volume

The amount of space contained by a 3-D shape is known as its "volume." Finding out the volume of a cuboid, which is a 3-D shape with rectangular sides, is easy. You simply multiply the length, width, and height (or depth) together.

A regular polyhedron has equal sides, equal angles, and equal faces. There are only five of them: the triangular pyramid, the cube, the octahedron, the dodecahedron and the icosahedron.

These role-playing dice contain four of the five of the regular polyhedrons. The set also contains other dice which are not regular polyhedrons, as they do not have equal sides and angles.

Regular polyhedrons are also called "Platonic solids" after the ancient Greek philosopher Plato.

DID YOU KNOW? Polyhedrons are often named after the number of sides they have. For example, an icosahedron has twenty sides, and the name comes from *eikosi*, the Greek word for "twenty."

HALL OF FAME: Plato

Plato was born in Athens around 428 BCE and died around 348 BCE. He's generally thought of as a philosopher, but he made important contributions to maths, and was especially interested in geometry. He believed that the five regular polyhedrons, which we call the "Platonic solids" after him, were the building blocks of the whole universe.

Gamers have their own names for these dice based on the number of sides. This shape is an icosahedron, but the die is called a "D20."

A sphere has the least possible surface area to enclose the maximum volume. It's a shape that appears a lot in nature, from bubbles to planets.

33

Scaling Up

Science fiction movies have shown nightmarish scenes of humans being attacked by giant ants, spiders, and even rabbits. But would we really have anything to fear from these creatures if they somehow grew in size? Probably not, according to maths.

Surface Area

It's all because surface area and volume don't get bigger at the same rate. If a mouse were scaled up to giant size, its surface area would get bigger, but its volume would get much, much bigger. The giant mouse wouldn't have enough skin to release the heat from its body, and it would overheat and die.

> Ants have thin legs to support their tiny weight. If they were scaled up, their volume would increase so much they'd need much thicker legs.

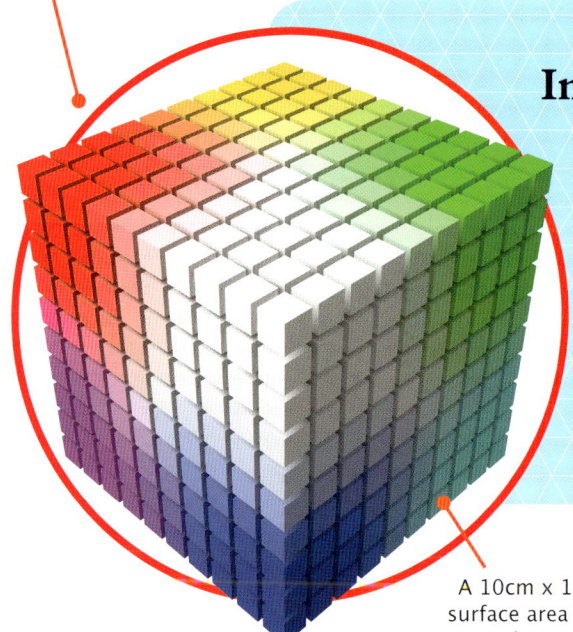

A 1cm x 1cm cube has a surface area of 6cm^2 and a volume of 1cm^3.

Increasing Volume

Imagine making the sides of a 1cm cube ten times longer. The surface area would become a hundred times bigger, and the volume would become a thousand times bigger. If you made an animal bigger, its volume would also increase at a different rate from its surface area.

A 10cm x 10cm cube has a surface area of 600cm^2 and a volume of 1,000cm^3.

DID YOU KNOW? Mathematicians measure the surface-area-to-volume ratio of shapes. A sphere has the lowest surface-area-to-volume ratio, while a shape with lots of spikes would have a very high one.

The internal organs of all creatures are optimized for their size. They couldn't function if you scaled up the animal.

Cats can fall from great heights unhurt. One reason is that they slow themselves down by splaying their legs, increasing their surface area and so creating more drag.

In reality, giant versions of animals and insects wouldn't be able to move, or even stay alive for very long.

Insects breathe through a network of tiny tubes. The giant ant's tubes wouldn't be able to provide enough oxygen for its huge new volume.

MATHS FACT: Surface Area and Volume

Length of cube in cm	Surface area of cube in cm²	Volume of cube in cm³
10	600	1,000
20	2,400	8,000
50	15,000	125,000
100	60,000	1,000,000

35

Pi

The distance around a circle is called the "circumference," and the distance across the middle is called the "diameter." Divide the circumference of a circle by the diameter and you'll get a number that is slightly over 3. This is pi, and it's one of the most famous numbers in the whole of maths.

An Irrational Number

Early estimates for pi were established in ancient Egypt and Babylon, and even referred to in the Bible. As the estimates got more accurate, it became clear that pi wasn't a simple number. The digits following the decimal place didn't end, or repeat themselves in a predictable pattern. Pi is called an "irrational number" because it can't be written as a simple fraction.

> If we know that the diameter of this pie is 20cm, we can work out the circumference using pi.

> The value of pi is approximately 3.14. We multiply this by the diameter of 20cm to find that the circumference is approximately 62.8cm.

> To find the area of the pie, we need to multiply the radius by itself and then multiply it by pi. So the area is approximately 314cm². This calculation is written as πr².

Decimal Places

The decimal digits of pi go on forever without any pattern. Naturally, this has made mathematicians compete with each other to see who can find the most accurate value of pi. The current record runs to over 31,000,000,000,000 digits. People also compete to memorize pi. The current champion recited pi to 70,000 places, which took him almost 10 hours.

> If you want to memorize pi, think of a sentence in which the number of letters in each word is equal to a digit of pi. For example, "How I wish I could recollect pi easily today" = 3.14159265

DID YOU KNOW? Maths lovers celebrate pi day every year on March 14th. This date is chosen because it can be written as 3/14.

HALL OF FAME: Archimedes

Archimedes was a Greek mathematician and engineer who lived in the third century BCE. He is famous for discovering the principle of displacement in his bathtub, shouting "Eureka!" and running naked through the town, although this story come from an account written long after his death. He also came up with a clever early estimate of pi by drawing 96-sided polygons inside and outside a circle.

circumference

diameter

The radius is the distance from the centre of the circle to the circumference. It is exactly half of the diameter.

radius

π

The sixteenth letter of the Greek alphabet, in lower case, is used as the symbol for pi. It's the first letter of the Greek word for "perimeter."

Symmetry

A 2-D shape or 3-D object has symmetry if it can be divided into identical pieces. We can find symmetry everywhere in nature, from flowers to faces. It also appears frequently in things designed by humans, such as buildings and vehicles.

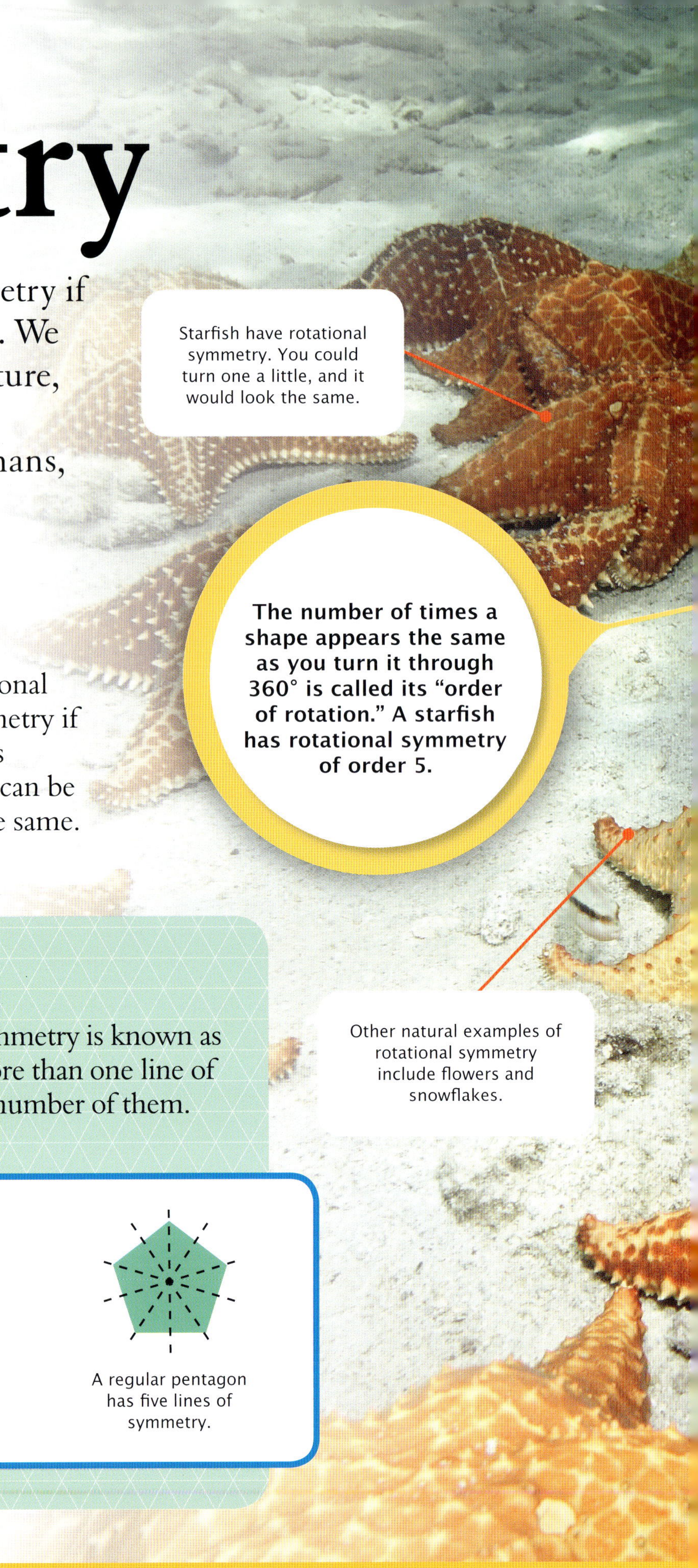

Starfish have rotational symmetry. You could turn one a little, and it would look the same.

The number of times a shape appears the same as you turn it through 360° is called its "order of rotation." A starfish has rotational symmetry of order 5.

Reflectional and Rotational

The two main types of symmetry are reflectional and rotational. A shape has reflectional symmetry if you can draw a line through it and both sides match. A shape has rotational symmetry if it can be rotated around a fixed point and still look the same.

Other natural examples of rotational symmetry include flowers and snowflakes.

Lines of Symmetry

A dividing line that marks reflectional symmetry is known as a "line of symmetry." Shapes can have more than one line of symmetry. In fact, a circle has an infinite number of them.

An equilateral triangle has three lines of symmetry.

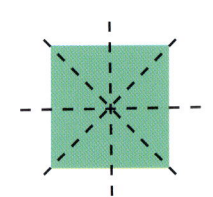

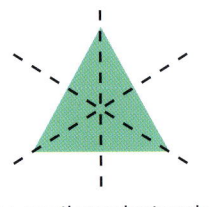

A square has four lines of symmetry.

A regular pentagon has five lines of symmetry.

DID YOU KNOW? Numbers can be symmetrical too. A number that remains the same when the digits are reversed is known as "palindromic." 02/02/2020 and 12/02/2021 were celebrated as palindromic dates.

Why do we think some people look beautiful? It could be to do with the amount of symmetry in their faces. Our features are never perfectly symmetrical, but some studies have found that faces that are closer to symmetry are deemed to be more attractive.

Several other creatures, such as sea urchins and sea cucumbers, have the same type of rotational symmetry as starfish.

MATHS FACT:
Orders of Symmetry

Order of rotational symmetry	Example of object
4	Jellyfish
5	Starfish
10	Dartboard
Infinite	Bubble

Topology

Topology looks at what happens to shapes as you bend, twist, and stretch them. It's sometimes called "rubber sheet geometry" because objects can be stretched like rubber, but not broken or stuck back together. In this different approach to geometry, the number of holes in a shape becomes very important.

Equivalent Shapes

If you can bend or stretch one shape into another, they're said to be "topologically equivalent." For example, a circle is topologically equivalent to a square but not a figure of eight, and a sphere is topologically equivalent to a glass but not a coffee cup.

According to topology, a coffee cup and a doughnut are the same shape.

The cup and the doughnut both have one hole. In the case of the coffee cup, it's in the handle, and in the case of the doughnut, it's in the middle.

HALL OF FAME: August Möbius

August Möbius was born in Germany in 1790 and died in 1868. He described the "Möbius strip" in 1858, although another German mathematician called Johann Listing was investigating the shape at the same time. Several other concepts in maths are named after him, including Möbius transformations, the Möbius plane, and the Möbius function. But the strip remains the most famous, and has inspired everyone from stage magicians to the Dutch artist M. C. Esher.

Möbius Strip

Topology has inspired mathematicians to investigate some very unusual shapes, such as the "Möbius strip." This is a bizarre shape with just one edge and one surface. An insect walking along it would cover both sides of the paper and come back to its starting point without crossing the edge.

It's easy to make your own Möbius strip. Take a strip of paper and make it into a loop. Give one end a 180° twist, then join the ends together.

You could pull and stretch the doughnut shape until it was the same as the coffee cup shape without tearing it or putting any bits back together.

Mathematicians would call the doughnut shape a "torus." A torus could also resemble a ring or a tyre, depending on how thick it is.

A pair of scissors has two holes, so it doesn't count as the same shape as a normal coffee cup in topology. But if the cup had two handles, it would be topologically equivalent to the scissors.

DID YOU KNOW? A German mathematician named Felix Klein came up with a shape that's even stranger than the Möbius strip. A "Klein bottle" is a 3-D shape with just one continuous side.

Fractals

Fractals are shapes that repeat their intricate patterns as you zoom in. These mesmerizing images are popular posters and screensavers. But fractals aren't just pretty. Over the last few decades, they've inspired a new branch of geometry that's influenced everything from medicine to engineering to economics.

Each bud of a Romanesco cauliflower is made up of similar smaller buds arranged in a spiral.

Natural Fractals

Many objects in nature display fractal patterns, such as coastlines, blood vessels, and cauliflowers. They may only be approximations of fractals rather than mathematically precise ones, but viewing them as fractals has been very useful to scientists.

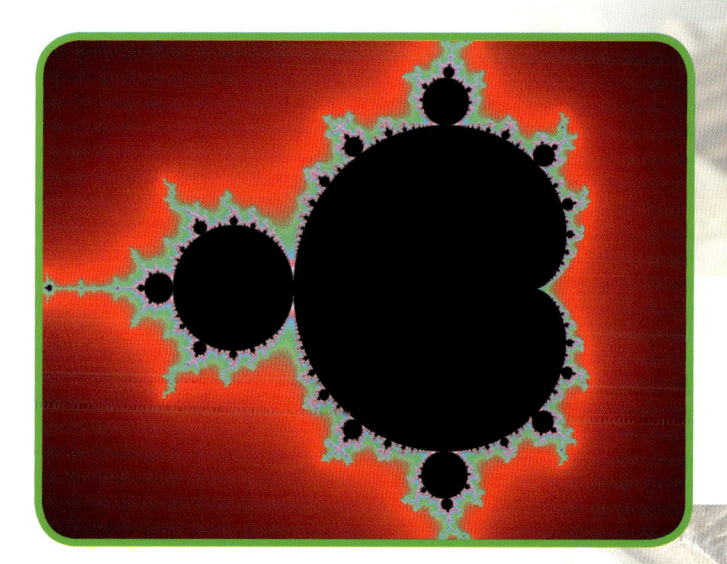

This fractal is called the "Mandelbrot set," after the Polish mathematician Benoit Mandelbrot. A complex equation is used to create a beautifully intricate pattern that repeats itself when magnified.

DID YOU KNOW? Computer animation companies such as Pixar use fractals to create realistic textures for things like fur and skin.

Fractals display "self-similarity." If you zoom in on the small parts, you'll find they resemble the whole thing.

The Sierpinski Triangle

This famous fractal design is named after the Polish mathematician Waclaw Sierpinski. You start with an equilateral triangle, divide it into four smaller ones, and remove the middle one. This leaves three smaller ones. Divide each of these and remove the middle ones again. Then repeat this over and over again to create the Sierpinski triangle.

These are the first steps in the sequence to construct the Sierpinski triangle.

Shapes found in nature are sometimes similar to computer-generated fractals. Computers create fractal images by repeating the same equation over and over again.

This is only an approximate fractal, because it eventually stops as you magnify it. Computer-generated fractals can go on forever.

HALL OF FAME: Benoit Mandelbrot

Benoit Mandelbrot was born in Poland in 1924 and died in the US in 2010. He worked as a researcher at the technology company IBM, which meant he had powerful computers to analyze the self-similar patterns that interested him. He coined the term "fractal," and published the influential book *The Fractal Geometry of Nature* in 1982.

Patterns in Nature

Some surprising mathematical patterns can be found in the natural world. Tessellation is when a geometric shape covers a flat surface. It might seem like something you'd only encounter at school, but you can actually find tessellating hexagons in beehives.

The hexagons used by bees to create honeycombs are both strong and mathematically efficient.

Spirals, Spots, and Stripes

Tessellation is just one of the patterns we can find in nature. There are also countless examples of spirals, symmetry, and fractals. Mathematicians have even looked for patterns in the spots of leopards and the stripes of zebras.

Alan Turing is best known for his work on early computers. But he also sought to explain how animals developed their distinctive spots, stripes, and blobs. These markings are now sometimes called "Turing patterns."

Bees make wax cells to store their honey. But building them takes energy, so they need a shape that will give them the most storage for the least wax.

MATHS FACT: Types of Patterns in Nature

Pattern	Natural Example
Reflectional symmetry	A butterfly's wings
Tessellation	Honeycomb
Spiral	Spiral galaxies
Fractal	Frost on glass
Meander	Bends in rivers

DID YOU KNOW? The Giant's Causeway in Northern Ireland is famous for its tessellating hexagonal rock columns. The shapes were formed millions of years ago when lava cooled and contracted.

Nautilus Shell

Spirals can be seen everywhere from goat horns to galaxies. Some people have claimed that many spirals in nature increase according to a number called "the golden ratio," which is approximately 1.618. But measuring the natural world will show that things don't quite fit to this precise pattern.

The circle is the shape that encloses the maximum area with the minimum perimeter, but this would leave gaps between the cells, which would have to be blocked with extra wax.

Shellfish have hard outer shells that spiral out from a central point. This nautilus half-shell is a famous example of a natural spiral.

Equilateral triangles, squares, and regular hexagons are the only regular polygons that tessellate. Of these three, the regular hexagon has the smallest perimeter, and will use the least wax. It's the perfect shape for honeycombs.

45

Chapter 3: Measurements

Distance

Humans have always needed to state how big things are or how far away they are. But it took a long time for measurements of distance to develop into standard units that could be used across different places. Ancient units like the cubit could vary wildly, causing a lot of confusion.

The Body

A cubit was commonly defined as the length from someone's elbow to the tip of their outstretched middle finger. Lots of other early types of measurement were based on parts of the body. Some of them are still in use today, as when we describe someone's height in "feet."

Metres are the standard international unit of distance. They are part of the "metric" system.

The barleycorn was used as a unit of length in medieval Britain. It was said to be a third of an inch, though real barleycorns vary in size.

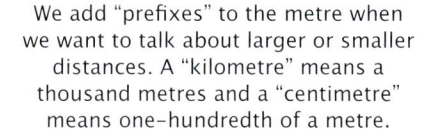

We add "prefixes" to the metre when we want to talk about larger or smaller distances. A "kilometre" means a thousand metres and a "centimetre" means one-hundredth of a metre.

DID YOU KNOW? The span of someone's outstretched arms is usually very similar to their height. Measure your own to see if they match up.

MATHS FACT: Measurements Based On the Body

Name	Definition
Cubit	The length of a human forearm
Foot	The length of a human foot
Hand	Distance across the palm and thumb
Finger	The width of a human finger
Pace	A full stride, from heel to heel

Road signs in countries such as the UK and US are written in miles instead of kilometres. These are known as "imperial" units.

If we didn't have the prefix "kilo," distance signs would be harder to read. 16,810 kilometres would have to be written as 16,810,000 metres.

Hands

The "hand" was once a popular measurement of distance. It was typically defined as the distance across the palm and thumb, with the fingers closed. It's still used today for measuring horses and ponies, and has been standardized as 4 inches, or 10.16 centimetres.

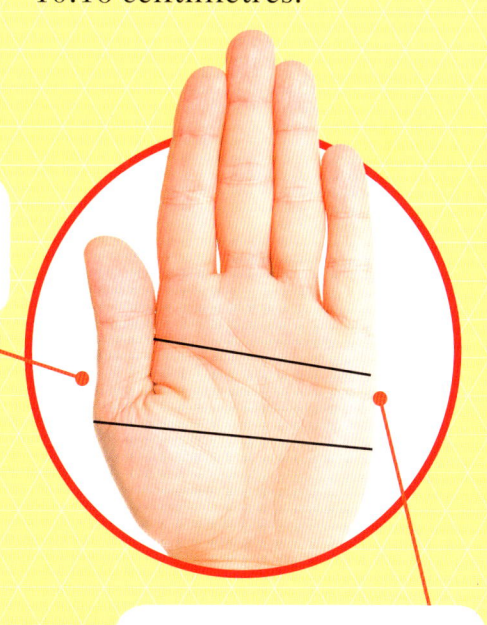

A "hand" was the distance across the palm and thumb.

A "palm" was a similar unit of measurement that didn't include the thumb.

47

Time

Early humans measured time by the sky. They could tell how much time had passed by the position of the Sun in the day, and the stars at night. But more precise ways of tracking time were eventually needed. The day was divided into hours, and clocks were designed to count how many had passed.

Sundials developed from the "shadow clocks" of ancient Egypt. These consisted of a raised bar that cast a shadow onto a lower one with hours marked on.

Ancient Number Systems

We divide days into 12 hours, hours into 60 minutes, and minutes into 60 seconds. This is because of the influence of the ancient Sumerians and Babylonians, who used number systems based around 12 and 60. This can be confusing when you're learning to tell the time, as most other measurements use base 10.

Some clocks use unusual methods to show how much time has passed. Water clocks measure the flow of water from one container to another, and candle clocks use evenly spaced notches in wax. There are even incense clocks (pictured) which release different scents so you can smell the time.

MATHS FACT: Units of Time

Name	Length
Nanosecond	0.000000001 seconds
Millisecond	0.001 seconds
Megasecond	1,000,000 seconds (about 1 week and 4.6 days)
Gigasecond	1,000,000,000 seconds (about 31.7 years)

Pendulum Clocks

Dutch scientist Christiaan Huygens devised the pendulum clock in 1656, and got a local clockmaker to build his design. Pendulum clocks use a swinging weight to keep time accurately, and remained popular until the early 20th century.

A weight at the end of a rod swings from side to side at a precise rate, rocking a small lever called an "escapement" and regulating the movement of the gears inside.

The part of a sundial that casts a shadow is known as a "gnomon."

The gnomon casts a shadow on the plate. As the Sun moves across the sky, the shadow lines up with the markings.

The hour lines are marked on the sundial's plate.

Sundials rely on sunlight to tell the time. They can't be used in cloudy weather or at night, so clocks that could be used in all conditions had to be developed.

DID YOU KNOW? Each town in the UK kept their own slightly different time until the widespread use of trains. A universal time was needed to schedule journeys, and it became known as "railway time."

49

Dates

The earliest calendars developed from humans observing the cycles of the moon. Keeping track of lunar cycles helped them with things like hunting animals and gathering fruit. Some places and structures that are believed to be prehistoric calendars have survived, such as a collection of 12 pits in Warren Field in Scotland.

Solar Years

More advanced calendars featuring days, months, and years were soon needed. But it wasn't going to be easy. A solar year, which is the amount of time it takes the Earth to orbit the Sun, is approximately 365 days, 5 hours, and 49 minutes. If you split a year into 365 days, the extra hours and minutes are going to mount up. It's a problem that took centuries to solve.

The Chinese calendar is lunisolar, which means it's divided according to the phases of the moon, but occasionally adjusted to fit the solar year.

Julius Caesar introduced a calendar with 365 days, and an extra day every fourth year, in 45 BCE. It was a big improvement over previous calendars, but it still wasn't totally accurate. It was out by a few minutes a year, and the minutes had built into days by the time the Gregorian Calendar was introduced in the 16th century.

MATHS FACT: Types of Calendar

Type	Meaning	Example
Solar	Based on movement of the Earth around the Sun	Gregorian Calendar
Lunar	Based on the cycles of the moon	Islamic Calendar
Lunisolar	Based on both the moon and the Sun	Chinese Calendar

DID YOU KNOW? If you're born on February 29th, you only have a birthday when it's a leap year. However, most people celebrate on February 28th or March 1st instead.

China has now adopted the Gregorian calendar for everyday life, but the traditional calendar still determines the dates of celebrations.

The moon takes 29 days, 12 hours, and 44 minutes to go through its full cycle. This doesn't multiply neatly into the 365 days, 5 hours, and 49 minutes of a solar year. The Chinese calendar sometimes has to add a 13th month to keep it in sync.

The Chinese New Year is celebrated on the first day of the year in the traditional calendar. This falls on the new moon that appears between January 21st and February 20th on the Gregorian calendar.

Leap Years

We now use the Gregorian Calendar, which was introduced by Pope Gregory XIII in 1582. It contains leap years, in which February includes an extra day. Leap years generally occur if a year is divisible by four. However, years such as 1900, 2000 and 2100 can only be leap years if they are divisible by 400.

Leap days help to keep our calendars lined up with solar years. The Earth takes slightly longer than 365 days to go around the Sun, and leap days make up for these hours.

51

Temperature

Measuring temperatures seems natural to us, but it took a long time for humans to assign numbers to levels of heat. The Greek physician Galen made an early attempt by mixing boiling water and ice to create a "neutral" temperature in the second century CE, and adding degrees of heat above and below it. But it wasn't until centuries later that major progress was made.

Thermoscopes

Several scientists in the late 16th century developed "thermoscopes." These were usually glass tubes in which liquids could rise and fall with temperature changes. These developed into the first thermometers, which added a numerical scale. A standard scale was needed to compare readings, but rival systems pioneered by Gabriel Fahrenheit and Anders Celsius both caught on.

Some of the most powerful supercomputers in the world are used to predict temperature.

Having an accurate forecast is vital for people who work on boats or in aircraft. Knowing exactly what the weather will be can even give the military an advantage in a conflict.

HALL OF FAME: Galileo Galilei

Galileo was one of the most important scientists in history. He lived in Italy from 1564 to 1642 and developed the thermoscope, the forerunner to the thermometer, as well as the military compass and the telescope. In the later years of his life he was sentenced to house arrest for supporting the idea that the planets move around the Sun, and the Earth is not the centre of the universe.

DID YOU KNOW? In the past, mercury was commonly used in thermometers. It has a freezing point of –39°C and a boiling point of 357°C, so it can measure a wide range of temperatures.

The satellites transmit their data to receiving stations on Earth. The data is sent to meteorologists, who use complex mathematical models to make forecasts.

Weather satellites orbiting the Earth measure microwave radiation in the atmosphere.

Galileo Thermometer

The Galileo Thermometer is an interesting alternative to the instruments we use today. Although it's named after Galileo Galilei, it wasn't actually invented by him. It was given his name because he discovered the principles on which it's based.

The cylinder contains clear liquid and a series of floats with different densities. The floats rise and fall as the temperature changes and the density of the clear liquid changes.

On windy days, it can feel much colder than the reading on a thermometer. You need to know the "wind chill," which takes into account the speed of the wind as well as the outside temperature.

53

Weight

Measuring the lightness and heaviness of objects was always important for trading goods. Hundreds of different measures were used, and their values varied from place to place. The kilogram was introduced in 1795, and was originally defined as the mass of one litre of water. It has now been adopted as the international standard unit.

Mass

It might seem as though the words "weight" and "mass" mean the same thing, but they're actually different. Mass is the amount of matter something contains, and weight is the pull of gravity on an object. The mass of an object is the same everywhere, but the weight changes with gravity. You would weigh less on the moon than you do on Earth.

It might seem surprising that a heavy container ship can stay afloat, yet a tiny stone will sink. But it can be explained by the ratio of an object's mass to its volume, which is called its "density."

Scales

We might think that scales tell us our weight, but they actually estimate our mass. They give a reading in kilograms, which is the standard unit for mass, and not Newtons, which is the standard unit for weight. The scales estimate our mass based on the downward force we're exerting.

The readings on scales swing back and forth as we step on and off them. This is because they're measuring downward force to work out mass.

DID YOU KNOW? If it were possible to weigh yourself on Jupiter, the scales would read two-and-a-half times as much.

HALL OF FAME: Isaac Newton

One of the greatest scientists who ever lived, Sir Isaac Newton was born in 1643 and died in 1727. He used maths to explain how objects move and how gravity affects them, and his work on planetary motion changed the way we see the universe. He pioneered a new branch of maths called "calculus," which studies how things change.

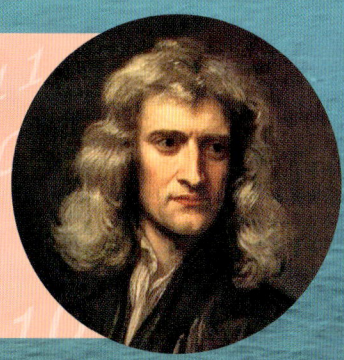

The density of water is about 1kg per litre. Anything with a lower density will float, and anything with a higher density will sink. Think about what would happen if a beach ball, which has a low density, and a bowling ball, which has a high density, were both thrown into water.

Objects on the moon experience about 16.6% of the gravity that they would on Earth. If you stepped on some scales on the moon, they would show only 16.6% of your weight on Earth.

The steel used to build the ship is very dense, but there is enough air in the whole vessel to make sure its overall density isn't too high.

Engineers have to make precise mathematical calculations when they're designing ships. They have to keep track of how things like the choice of building materials will affect the ship's density.

55

SI Units

Standard measurements that are the same everywhere have always been needed. But it wasn't until 1960 that an international system of units was agreed. These are known as "SI" Units, which stands for the French words "Système International."

Seven Standard Units

The system introduced seven units that are accepted across the world—the metre for distance, the kilogram for mass, the second for time, the ampere for electric current, the kelvin for temperature, the mole for the amount of a substance, and the candela for luminous intensity. These units are used globally for science, technology, and business.

The metre is the SI unit for distance. It's used in sporting events such as sprint races.

Prefixes

All seven SI units can be scaled up and down by adding the same "prefixes." These are added to the beginning of the units to make new ones. For example, "kilo-" is used for thousands, and "centi-" is used for hundredths, as in kilometres and centimetres.

A kilogram is a thousand grams. A milligram is a thousandth of a gram.

Short races like the 100 metres can be run in a straight line, but longer ones such as the 200 metres have to follow the curve of the track. If they all started from the same place, the runners on the inside track would have less distance to cover. So the athletes start at different points.

DID YOU KNOW? A nanosecond is a billionth of a second. Light travels approximately 30 centimetres in a nanosecond.

MATHS FACT: SI Prefixes

Prefix	Meaning	Decimal
Kilo	Thousand	1000
Hecto	Hundred	100
Deca	Ten	10
Deci	Tenth	0.10
Centi	Hundredth	0.01
Milli	Thousandth	0.001

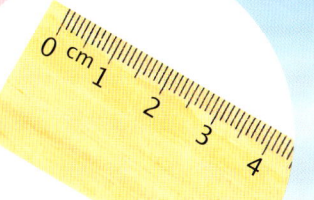

The metre was was originally defined as one ten-millionth of the distance from the North Pole to the equator.

The metre was part of the "metric system" that was adopted in France in 1799. It was meant to replace the chaotic array of measurements that were being used at the time.

The SI unit for measuring electric currents is called the "ampere," which is often shortened to "amp." Electric current is measured with an ammeter.

Money

Money plays such an important role in our lives that it's hard to imagine a time when it didn't exist. But early humans would have used a system of "bartering." This means trading goods such as cattle, sheep, grain, and tools. But it wasn't always easy to find someone who had what you wanted and needed what you had.

Tokens of Exchange

The development of numbers and counting meant that money could be introduced. Tokens of exchange were made from clay, bamboo, and leather. Precious metals were used, and the first coins were made. Notes of credit developed into banknotes that saved people from carrying lots of coins around. And in our era, credit cards and online transactions often replace physical money.

Coins meant that people could move away from swapping goods for other goods.

Originally, pieces of metal were traded because they could be used for things like toolmaking. These eventually developed into coins, which held a value that had nothing to do with their usefulness as objects.

Inflation

Prices go up over time. A chocolate bar that costs a pound today might only have cost a few pence when your grandparents were young. This is known as "inflation." Costs usually go up over such a long period of time that you don't really notice it, but a very high rate of inflation can cause a currency to lose its value.

Germany in the 1920s suffered hyperinflation. By the end of 1923, the US dollar was worth 42 trillion German marks.

Coins store value. If you were holding on to a surplus of food for trading, it would eventually rot. But if you sold it for coins, the value would last for much longer.

DID YOU KNOW? Interest can work in your favour if you're a saver. If you paid £1,000 into a bank account that pays 5% interest, you'd get £50 at the end of the year.

If you wanted to borrow money to buy something like a house, you'd have to pay it all back, plus some extra known as "interest." The total cost you end up paying for something can be much higher when you take interest into account.

Coins have been used for hundreds of years, but they might not be around for much longer. The move to electronic payments means they could soon disappear.

MATHS FACT: Interest Rates and True Cost

Cost of house	Annual interest rate	Term	Total amount paid
£250,000	2%	30 Years	£400,000
£250,000	3%	30 Years	£475,000
£250,000	4%	30 Years	£550,000

59

Motion

Anyone who's ever been in a car will be familiar with how motion is measured. Speed limits such as "40 kilometres per hour" tell you how fast you can drive and the speedometre tells you how fast you're currently going. If you travel at exactly 40 kilometres for one hour, you'll have travelled 40 kilometres. But in maths and physics, motion is measured not just as speed, but as velocity.

Speed and Velocity

Speed measures how fast something moves. Velocity measures how fast something moves in a particular direction. If we say the car is travelling at 40 kilometres an hour, we're giving a speed. But if we say it's travelling at 40 kilometres an hour northwards, we're giving a velocity. Speed is called a "scalar" quantity, because it has magnitude, or size. Velocity is called a "vector" quantity, because it has magnitude and direction.

The wind makes a big difference to the speed of an aircraft. A "headwind" slows it down, while a "tailwind" pushes it along. This is why you sometimes arrive earlier than expected.

An aircraft is in the "cruise" phase of flight after it has climbed and before it descends. The typical cruising speed of a commercial airliner is around 900 kilometres per hour.

MATHS FACT: Top Speeds

Peregrine falcon	350 km/h
Sailfish	110 km/h
Cheetah	100 km/h
Human	35 km/h
Sloth	0.25 km/h

Speedometres show instantaneous speed, which is how fast we're travelling at a particular moment. We might complete a journey at an average speed of 30 kilometres per hour. But along the way, we might have had an instantaneous speed of 60 kilometres per hour on a motorway, and 0 kilometres per hour at traffic lights.

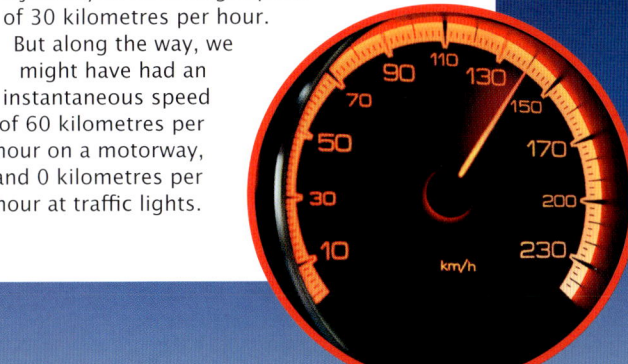

A flight from Europe to the USA might have a speed of 760 km/h, and a velocity of 760 km/h west.

The plane might be placed in a holding pattern, circling in the air while it waits for a runway to become available. Its speed could be constant, but its velocity would be changing all the time, because it would keep changing direction.

Displacement

Because velocity takes direction into account, it measures displacement rather than distance. This is an important distinction. For example, a formula one car could be hurtling around a track at 200 kilometres per hour. But because it ends up exactly where it started, it has no displacement, and its overall velocity is zero.

An object such as this racing car could have a very high speed, but a velocity of zero.

DID YOU KNOW? The Earth is constantly spinning and moving around the Sun, and our solar system is constantly zooming around our galaxy. So you are effectively in motion all the time.

Light Years

The light year is a measurement that lets scientists deal with the huge numbers that turn up when you study the universe. Despite the name, a light year is a measure of distance rather than time. It's the distance that light travels in a year, which is approximately 9.5 trillion kilometres.

Time and Distance

It might seem strange to measure distance by referring to time. But it's something we do in everyday life too. We might say that the town centre is a 20-minute drive away, or that we live five minutes away from our school. The difference with light years is that the distances are so huge, we needed a new type of measurement to cope with them.

> Light years are so vast that even the Sun isn't a light year away from Earth. In fact, it's only 8.3 light minutes away.

> The Sun is 149,597,870,700 metres away from Earth. This is sometimes called an "Astronomical Unit" or "AU," and is used to measure distances within the solar system.

The NASA Infrared Telescope Facility is built on top of the volcano Mauna Kea in Hawaii. Powerful telescopes like this let scientists study parts of the universe that are many light years away.

DID YOU KNOW? The mean distance from the Earth to the Moon is approximately 1.28 light seconds.

The closest star to Earth, other than the Sun, is Proxima Centauri, which is 4.2 light years away.

Light Seconds

Light travels at 299,792,458 metres a second. This is known as a "light-second." You can multiply it by 60 to get a light minute. Then multiply that by 60 to get a light hour. Then multiply that by 24 to get a light day. And finally, multiply that by 365.25 to get a light year.

A light second is 299,792,458 metres. So a light year in metres is 299,792,458 × 60 × 60 × 24 × 365.25, which is 9,460,730,472,580,800.

The Astronomical Unit is the mean distance from the centre of the Earth to the centre of the Sun. The Earth's orbit is an ellipse rather than a perfect circle, meaning it's sometimes closer to the Sun, and sometimes further away.

MATHS FACT: Distances of Other Stars From the Sun

Name of Star	Approximate Distance in Light Years
Proxima Centauri	4.2
Barnard's Star	6.0
Wolf 359	7.9
Lalande 21185	8.3

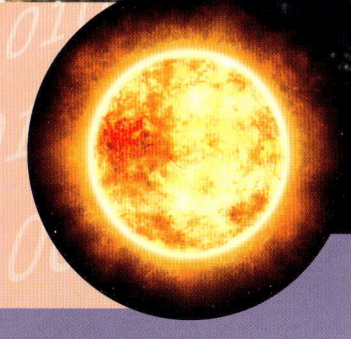

63

Maps

Sometimes it's hard to describe exactly where something is. It's much easier to grab a piece of paper and scribble down a diagram. If you do this, you'll have created a basic kind of map. But if a map is going to be truly useful, it needs to show accurate distances between things.

This arrow shows which way north is. We can use a compass to make sure we're going in the right direction.

Scale

Maps are drawn to scale, which means that a certain distance on the map is equal to a certain distance in the real world. The scale of a map is written as a ratio, such as 1:25,000. This means that every 1cm on the map represents 25,000 cm, or 250 metres. Maps that are used for different purposes have different scales. For example, a 1:25,000 scale would be good for hiking, but 1:200,000 would be more appropriate for a road atlas.

The needle in a compass aligns with the Earth's magnetic field to show direction. As well as the directions north, east, south, and west, compasses often show degree markings. North corresponds to 0°, East to 90°, South to 180°, and West to 270°.

HALL OF FAME: René Descartes

René Descartes was a French philosopher, mathematician, and scientist who was born in 1596 and died in 1650. His pioneering ideas about co-ordinates were first published as an appendix to a philosophical work in 1637. He was also behind several other important mathematical developments, such as using letters to represent known and unknown quantities in equations.

1:1,000,000

This ratio is the scale of the map. It means that 1cm on the map is equal to 1,000,000cm in the real world—which is 10,000m or 10km. So if you measure the distance from Badajoz to Mérida as 6cm, that means the real distance is 60km.

Some maps have contour lines. These join up points that are an equal height above sea level. They are important if you're walking across hills and mountains.

Maps have horizontal and vertical lines known as "grid lines." On this map, they're 10cm apart. We know from the scale that there are 100km between each grid line in the real world, so it makes distances easy to judge.

Co-ordinates

The French mathematician René Descartes came up with a famous system to describe where something is using numbers, called "co-ordinates." Based on a starting point of 0, the co-ordinates tell you how far left or right something is, then how far up and down it is. Co-ordinates are used to pinpoint precise locations on maps.

y-axis

This mark is four across from 0, and 2 up from 0. We write the location as (4,2).

x-axis

DID YOU KNOW? The grids on maps are often numbered. A co-ordinate that gives a precise location on a map is called a "grid reference."

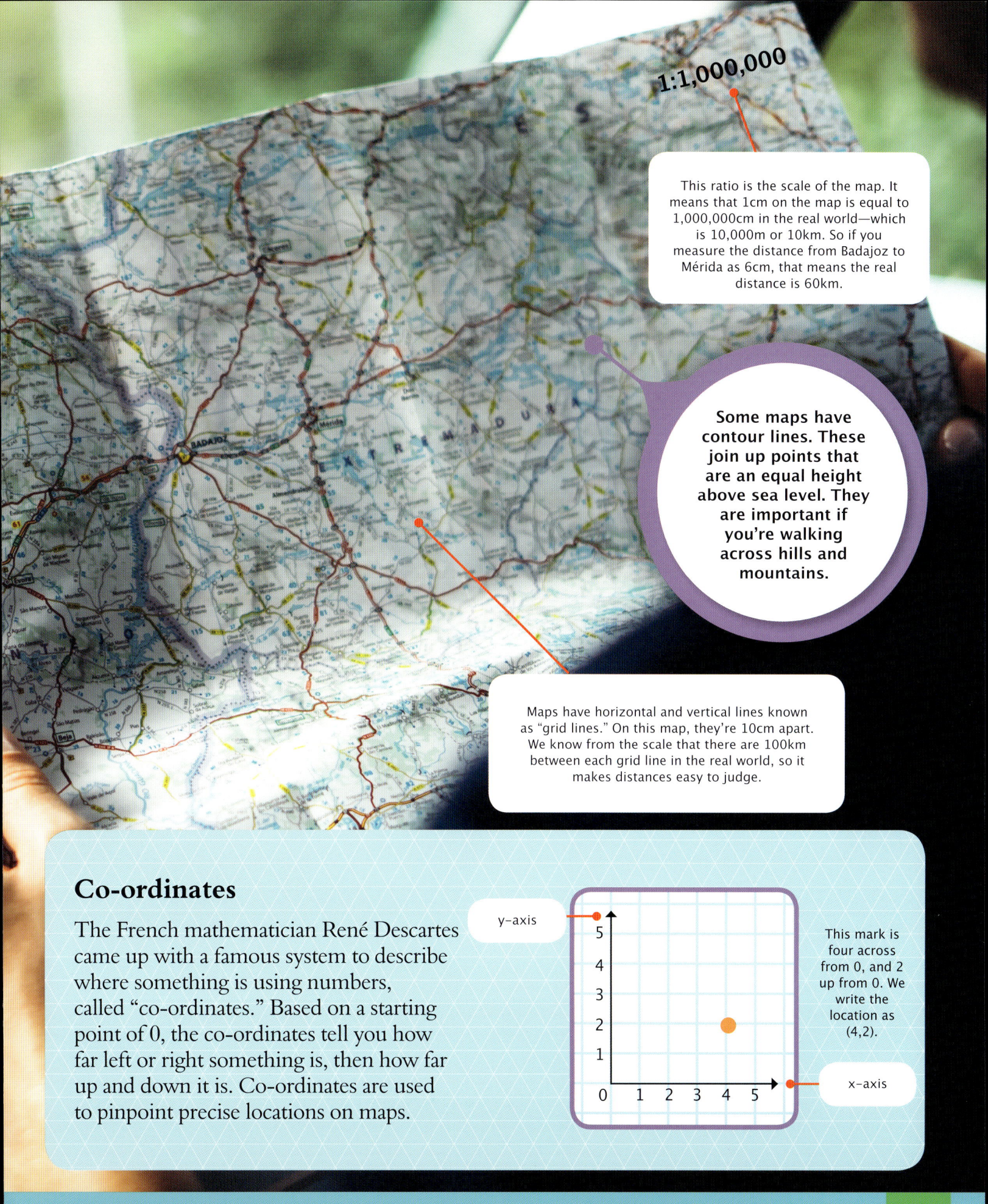

65

Chapter 4: Statistics and Probability

Data

Data has never been more important. Our behaviour is constantly being reduced to numbers that record everything from our shopping habits to our taste in music. In a world of non-stop online activity, data has become a precious resource. There's never been a more vital time to understand how data is gathered and presented.

Statistics

Statistics is the branch of maths that deals with collecting and analyzing data. It finds simple ways of showing it, and searches for patterns and links. It also looks at how data changes over time, so we can predict what will happen next.

The group you're studying is called the "population." If you collect data from the whole of a population, it's called a "census." If you collect data from part of it, it's called a "sample."

When individuals are chosen from a population by chance, it's known as "random sampling." Imagine if you put the names of everyone from your school into a hat and pulled out ten. You'd have created a random sample.

MATHS FACT: Types of Sampling

Random Sampling	Choosing individuals by chance.
Systematic Sampling	Following a system such as every fifth person to enter a supermarket, or every third house on a street.
Stratified Sampling	Breaking the population into groups based on things like age and gender, then randomly sampling from each group.
Cluster Sampling	Breaking the population into groups, then randomly sampling whole groups.

The Age of Data

Data is incredibly valuable in the modern digital world. Companies want to know a lot about their customers so they can develop new products and services, decide how much to charge for them, and how to advertise them.

Every time you search online, browse a shopping site, or even choose a video to watch, you are creating data that can be very useful to companies.

Expressing data as a percentage can make it easy to understand. For example, you might ask a sample of 36 pupils if they cycle in, and 9 might say yes. You could express your finding as "25% of students cycle to school."

When people volunteer to give data, it can lead to "self-selection bias." For example, people with very strong opinions on a topic are much more likely to vote in online polls.

A sample is biased when it doesn't truly represent a larger population. For example, sampling 12-year-old school students to find out about all 12-year-olds is biased, because it doesn't include the home-schooled.

DID YOU KNOW? Quantitative data deals with numbers, and qualitative data deals with descriptions, such as what colour something is.

67

Averages

Giving the average value of a data set can help us understand it. Telling someone that the average adult spends three hours using their phone every day would be more engaging than showing them a list of all the times collected in a survey. But there are different ways of working out an average, and it's important to be clear about which one is being used.

Mean, Median, and Mode

If you add all the numbers in a data set, and divide the total by the number of values, you'll get the "mean" value. If you list all the numbers in order, the one is the middle is the "median." And the "mode" is the number that appears most frequently. The mean, median, and mode can all be different for the same set of data.

> Measure the heights of everyone in your class. If you add all the results together and divide them by the number of pupils, you'll get the mean height.

Outliers

Imagine you were trying to find the average length of a particular train journey. You could record the times for a week, add them all together, then divide them by seven to get the mean time. But if the train were severely delayed one day, it would make the mean very misleading. You could use the median or mode instead, or view the delayed time as an "outlier" and exclude it from the calculation.

If the mean journey time was 20 minutes for the first six days, an "outlier" result of 1 hour and 20 minutes for the seventh day would change the mean to 28 minutes and 34 seconds.

DID YOU KNOW? If a data set has two modes, it is known as "bimodal."

68

The mode is the value that appears the most. Two or more pupils in your sample could have the same height, which would be the mode for your data.

If someone from your class is much taller than the others, they would make the mean height much higher. In such cases, the median or mode could be more useful.

List the heights in order and the median will be in the middle. If there are two middle values, add them and divide the total by two to get the median.

MATHS FACT: Mean, Median, and Mode

Data Set	3, 4, 6, 6, 7, 10, 11, 12, 13
Mean	Add the numbers and divide by 9 to get 8
Median	The number in the middle when they're written in order is 7
Mode	The most frequent number is 6

Correlation

If two sets of data are strongly linked, we say they have high correlation. If there is a link, but not a very strong one, we say they have low correlation. If there's no link at all, we say they have no correlation. It's easy to imagine which sets of data ought to have a high correlation, such as the length of someone's hair and the amount of shampoo they use, and which ought to have no correlation, such as the size of someone's shoes and the amount of shampoo they use.

Causation

It's often said that "correlation is not causation." This means that a high correlation between two sets of data doesn't prove that one thing causes the other. For example, you might find that there's a high correlation between the sales of sunglasses and the sales of ice cream. This doesn't mean that wearing sunglasses makes you want to eat ice cream.

If you wanted to find out if there was a correlation between snowfall and sledge sales, you could track both sets of data. It's likely that you would find a strong positive correlation.

Scatter Graphs

Plotting data onto a scatter graph is a simple way to show the relationship between the variables shown on the x-axis and the y-axis.

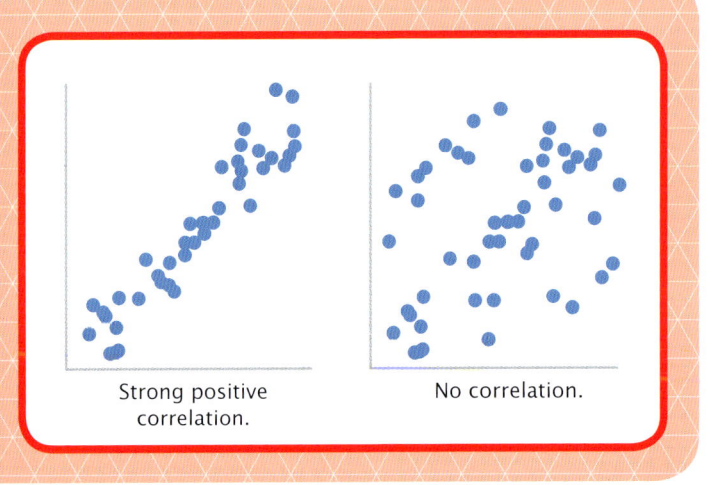

Strong positive correlation.

No correlation.

DID YOU KNOW? Many correlations that happened purely by chance have been collected by statisticians. For example, there was once a strong positive correlation between divorce rates and margarine sales.

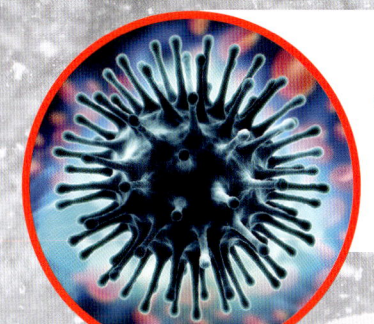

The sales of hats and sledges correlate because they are both caused by another thing—snowfall. But sometimes data sets correlate by chance.

Negative correlation means that one value decreases as another increases. For example, there is a strong negative correlation between cases of flu and the number of people who have been vaccinated against it.

You could also compare sales data for woolly hats and sledges. It's likely that you would also find a strong positive correlation, but this does not mean that wearing hats makes people want to buy sledges.

MATHS FACT: Examples of Correlation

First Variable	Second Variable	Correlation
Time spent running	Number of calories burned	Positive
Number of sweets you get to eat	Number of friends you share them with	Negative
Temperature on Mars	Number of pupils achieving the top grade in maths	None

71

Frequency

Frequency is the number of times a particular value occurs. For example, if you were measuring the heights of everyone in your class, and you found that three of them were 150cm, you could say that this height had a frequency of 3. Frequency is often recorded using a tally and presented in a "frequency distribution table."

> You would assume that a number taken from a real-life data set has an equal chance of starting with 1, 2, 3, 4, 5, 6, 7, 8, or 9. In fact, there's a 30% chance that it starts with 1. The surprising frequency of leading digits is known as "Benford's law."

Benford's Law

Studying frequency in data can reveal some surprising patterns. One of the most famous is known as "Benford's law." This is named after an engineer called Frank Benford, who noticed that in many sets of data, the most common digit that a number starts with is 1. The second most common is 2, the third most common is 3, and so on.

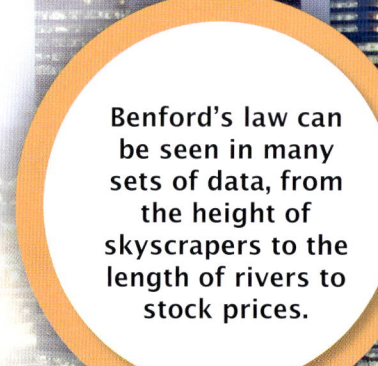

> Benford's law can be seen in many sets of data, from the height of skyscrapers to the length of rivers to stock prices.

Frequency Distribution Tables

It's sometimes useful to count how often values occur in a data set and gather them in a table. For example, your favourite football team could have scored the following number of goals in the season so far: 1, 4, 2, 2, 0, 1, 3, 1, 0, 1. They scored four goals once, three goals once, two goals twice, no goals twice, and one goal four times. This is how the data would look in a frequency distribution table:

Score	Frequency
0	2
1	4
2	2
3	1
4	1

> Frequency distribution tables can help us digest data.

MATHS FACT: Benford's Law Table

Digit	Probability it will be the first digit	Digit	Probability it will be the first digit
1	30.1%	6	6.7%
2	17.6%	7	5.8%
3	12.5%	8	5.1%
4	9.7%	9	4.6%
5	7.9%		

Benford's law can be used to fight crime. A set of data that has been made up is unlikely to follow it. So figures that don't conform to Benford's Law could be suspicious.

Criminal investigators check the data of companies to see if they match the pattern predicted by Benford's law. If they don't, it could be a sign that they're committing fraud.

Benford's law has been used to detect fraud in elections. Voting data has been analyzed to see if it looks like the results were made up. Unsurprisingly, this has been very controversial.

DID YOU KNOW? Sorting data into groups like 0-5 and 5-10 can be useful when making a frequency distribution table.

Graphs

Once data has been gathered, it needs to be presented. Diagrams such as graphs and charts can make it easy to take in. But there are many different types of diagram, and it's important to choose the best one for your findings.

Line Graphs

Line graphs are useful for displaying data that changes over time. Time can be shown on the horizontal scale (called the "x-axis") and another variable such as temperature can be shown on the vertical scale (called the "y-axis"). The graph is created by drawing a dot for each data value, and then joining them with straight lines.

AVERAGE TEMPERATURE IN LONDON

The y-axis can show a variable such as temperature, population, rainfall, sales, or anything else you've gathered information about.

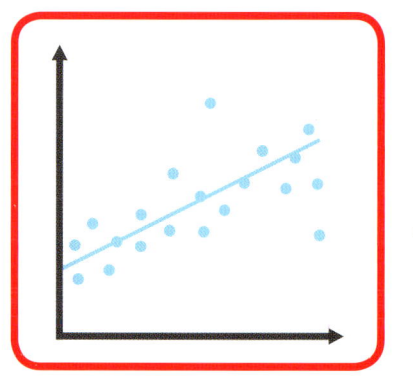

The data that has been collected, in this case the average temperatures for each month, is plotted onto the graph.

Rather than joining every dot on a graph, you can draw a "line of best fit" through as many as possible.

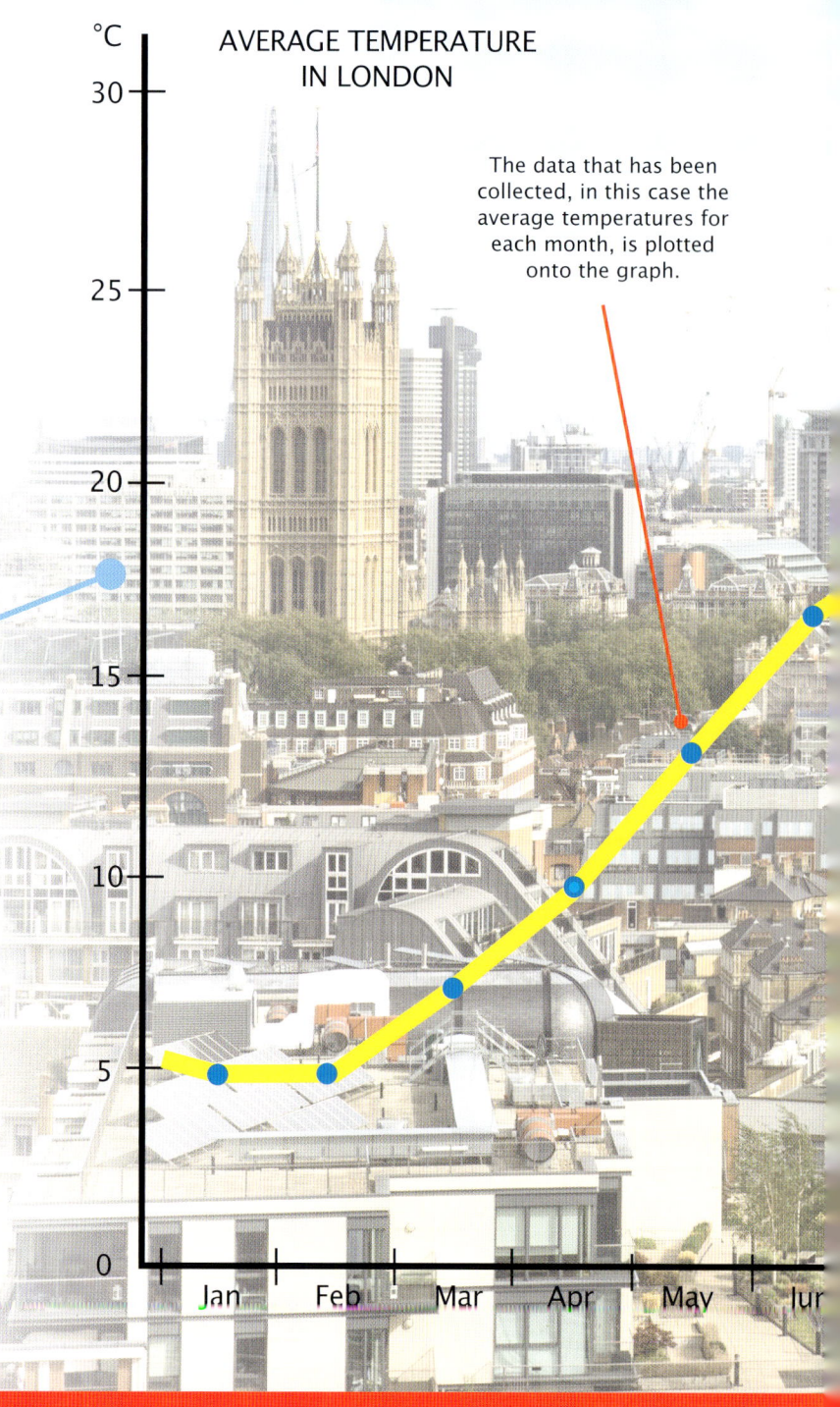

DID YOU KNOW? You can use the patterns shown by graphs to predict future data. This is called "extrapolation."

MATHS FACT: Graphs Need S.A.L.T.

Scale	Choose scales that will show your data accurately.
Axes	Mark the scale in even increments on each axis.
Label	Label each axis with the type of data and unit.
Title	The title should explain the purpose of the graph.

Manipulating Data

These graphs show the same data of average global temperature by year. But the scale of the y-axis is different. On the first graph, it looks as if there has been little change in temperature, while the second graph shows a definite rise.

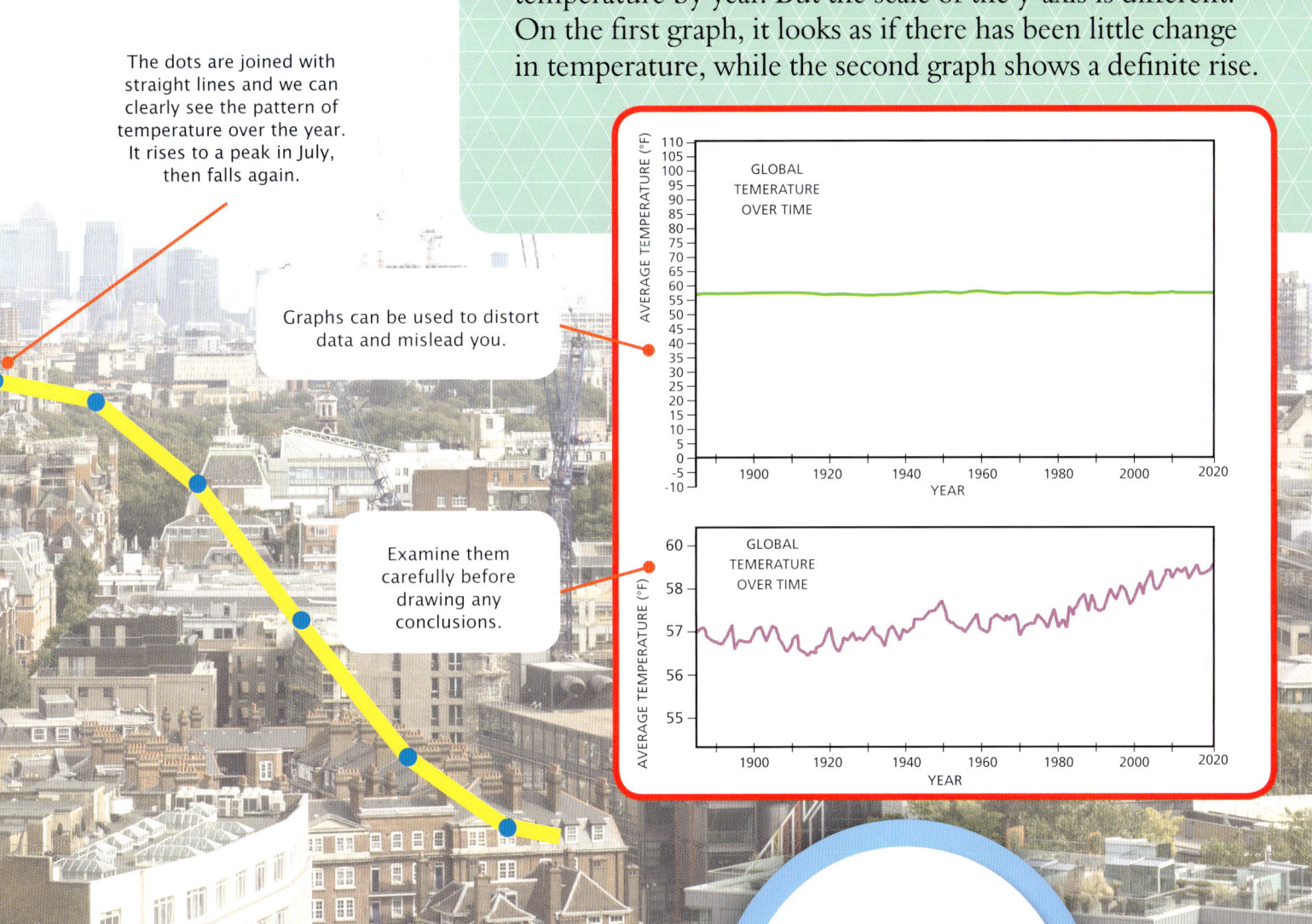

The dots are joined with straight lines and we can clearly see the pattern of temperature over the year. It rises to a peak in July, then falls again.

Graphs can be used to distort data and mislead you.

Examine them carefully before drawing any conclusions.

The x-axis can be used to show time. This can be in years, months, weeks, minutes, or even seconds, depending on the data.

75

Charts

While line graphs might be good for showing how things change over time, other diagrams are more suited to different data sets. For example, what if you found out how everyone in your class travels to school and wanted to present your findings? It would be confusing to plot the results on a graph and draw a line through them. A bar chart would suit them much better.

Bar Charts

Bar charts are useful when you're presenting data in separate categories. In the example of getting to school, the categories could be "car," "walk," "bus," and "bike." A separate bar could be drawn for each, and the height of the bars would tell you how many pupils use each one. There are many other types of chart, and they all have particular strengths. For example, a pie chart is good for showing relative sizes in a data set.

In the middle of the 19th century, Florence Nightingale proved that you could change the world with charts, and it was all to do with the cleanliness of hospitals.

During the Crimean War, hundreds of soldiers were dying in military hospitals. Many assumed this was because of their battle injuries, but Nightingale decided to record all the causes of death.

HALL OF FAME: Florence Nightingale

Florence Nightingale was born in 1820 and died in 1910. It's sometimes said that she invented the pie chart. This isn't true, as William Playfair had published some in 1801. But Nightingale made the diagrams popular, and showed how well they could communicate data. And she did come up with a variation of the pie chart known as the "polar area diagram."

DID YOU KNOW? A pictogram is a chart that uses simple pictures to represent data.

Venn Diagrams

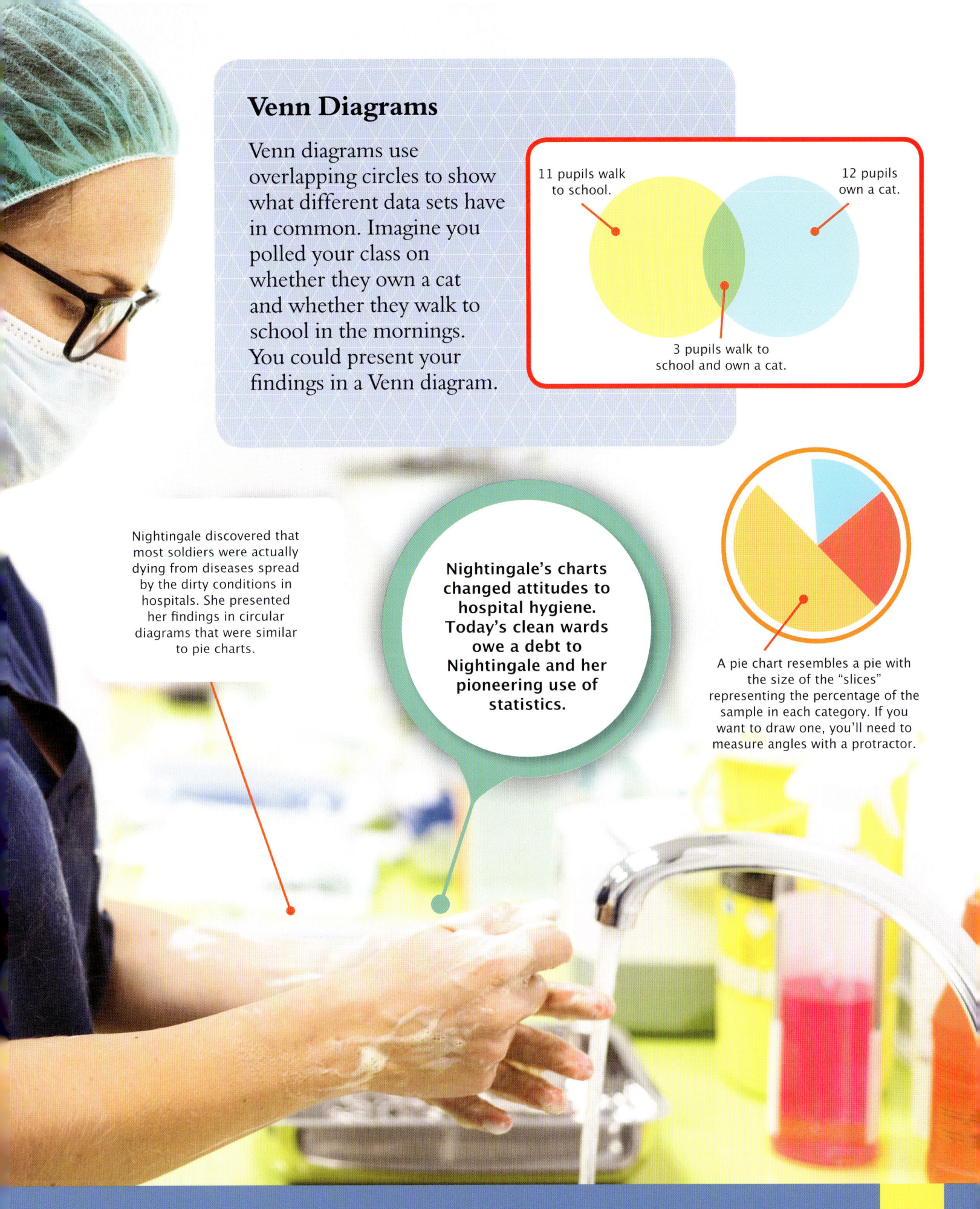

Venn diagrams use overlapping circles to show what different data sets have in common. Imagine you polled your class on whether they own a cat and whether they walk to school in the mornings. You could present your findings in a Venn diagram.

11 pupils walk to school.

12 pupils own a cat.

3 pupils walk to school and own a cat.

Nightingale discovered that most soldiers were actually dying from diseases spread by the dirty conditions in hospitals. She presented her findings in circular diagrams that were similar to pie charts.

Nightingale's charts changed attitudes to hospital hygiene. Today's clean wards owe a debt to Nightingale and her pioneering use of statistics.

A pie chart resembles a pie with the size of the "slices" representing the percentage of the sample in each category. If you want to draw one, you'll need to measure angles with a protractor.

77

Growth

Many sets of data will show steady growth, while others will display sudden and rapid growth that is called "exponential." For example, you might study the size of a population of bacteria and find that it's doubling every hour. You could say it was growing "exponentially."

Exponential growth soon leads to enormous numbers, as shown in a famous Indian legend.

Linear and Exponential

When something grows at a constant rate, it is known as "linear growth." If you saved £1 a day, you would have £1, then £2, then £3, then £4, and so on. When something grows in relation to its current value, such as doubling, it's known as "exponential growth." If you doubled your savings every day, you would have £1, then £2, then £4, then £8, and so on.

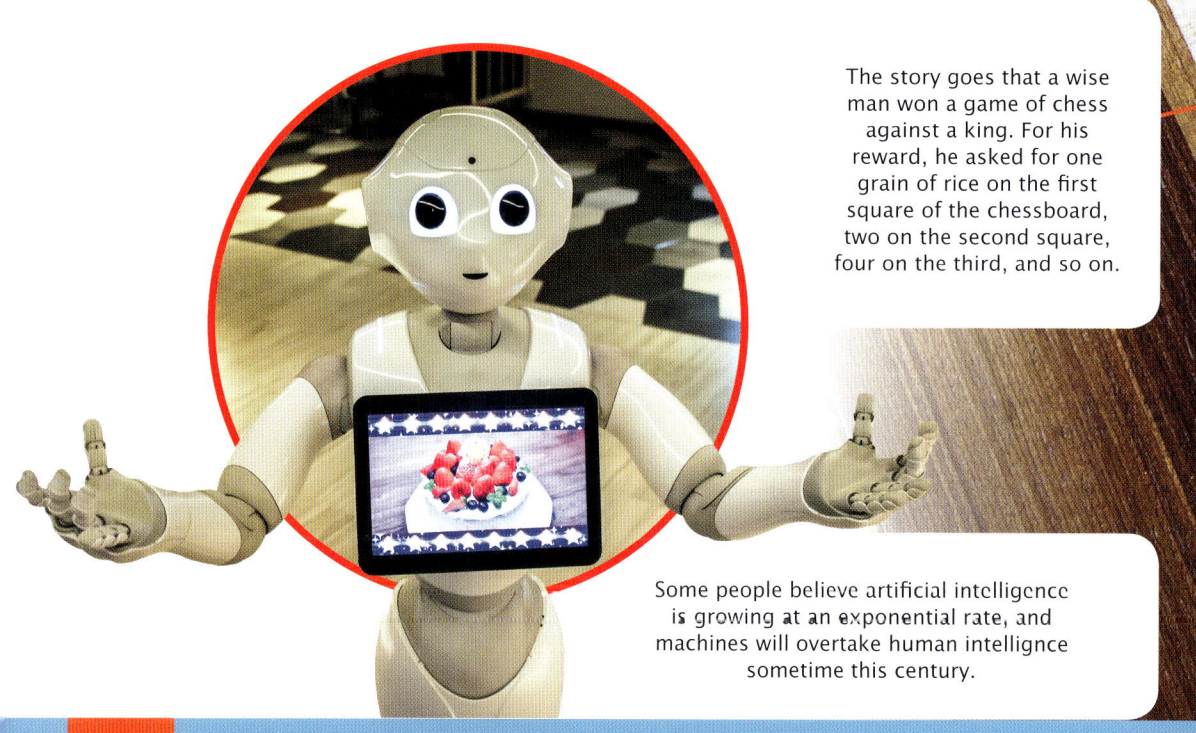

The story goes that a wise man won a game of chess against a king. For his reward, he asked for one grain of rice on the first square of the chessboard, two on the second square, four on the third, and so on.

Some people believe artificial intelligence is growing at an exponential rate, and machines will overtake human intelligence sometime this century.

DID YOU KNOW? Decreasing at an exponential rate is known as "exponential decay."

Plotting Growth

You can see the dramatic difference between linear and exponential growth if you plot them on a graph. Linear growth looks like a straight diagonal line, while exponential growth leads to a steep curve.

The number of rice grains double every time. The sequence begins 1, 2, 4, 8, 16, 32, 64, 128... but soon gets into millions and billions.

The king agreed, but eventually realized he would owe the wise man over 18 quintillion grains in total. The story shows how our minds are used to linear growth, and the results of exponential growth can be a shock.

MATHS FACT: Doubling Your Money

Day	Amount	Day	Amount
1	£0.01	10	£5.12
2	£0.02	20	£5,242.88
3	£0.04	30	£5,368,709.12
4	£0.08	40	£5,497,558,138.88

Probability

Maths can't tell you exactly what will happen in the future, but it can help you work out how likely something is. Probability looks at the chances of things happening. It is often written as a number between 0 and 1, with 0 meaning something is impossible, and 1 meaning something is certain.

Total Outcomes

You can work out probability by dividing the number of ways an event can happen by the total number of outcomes. For example, if you deal a card, the chance of it being the ace of spades is 1 out of 52, or 0.01923. There are 52 outcomes, but only one way that particular event can happen. The chance of the card being an ace of any suit is 4 out of 52, or 0.07692. There are 52 outcomes again, but this time there are four ways the event can happen.

If you roll a die, the chance of getting a six is 1 out of 6, or 0.16667. There are six outcomes, and only one way the event can happen.

If you roll a die, the chance of getting an odd number is 1 out of 2, or 0.5. There are six outcomes, and three ways the event can happen.

HALL OF FAME: Pierre De Fermat

Pierre de Fermat was a French mathematician who was born in 1607 and died in 1665. Along with Blaise Pascal, he developed the theory of probability, applying maths to things such as dice games. He is also remembered for a statement that puzzled mathematicians for centuries. He wrote that he could prove a mathematical statement, but he didn't say how. The puzzle became known as "Fermat's last theorem," and it was only solved in 1985.

DID YOU KNOW? The sum of the probabilities for all possible outcomes should be 1. The chance of a coin landing on heads is 0.5. The chance of coin landing on tails is 0.5. The sum of these is 1.

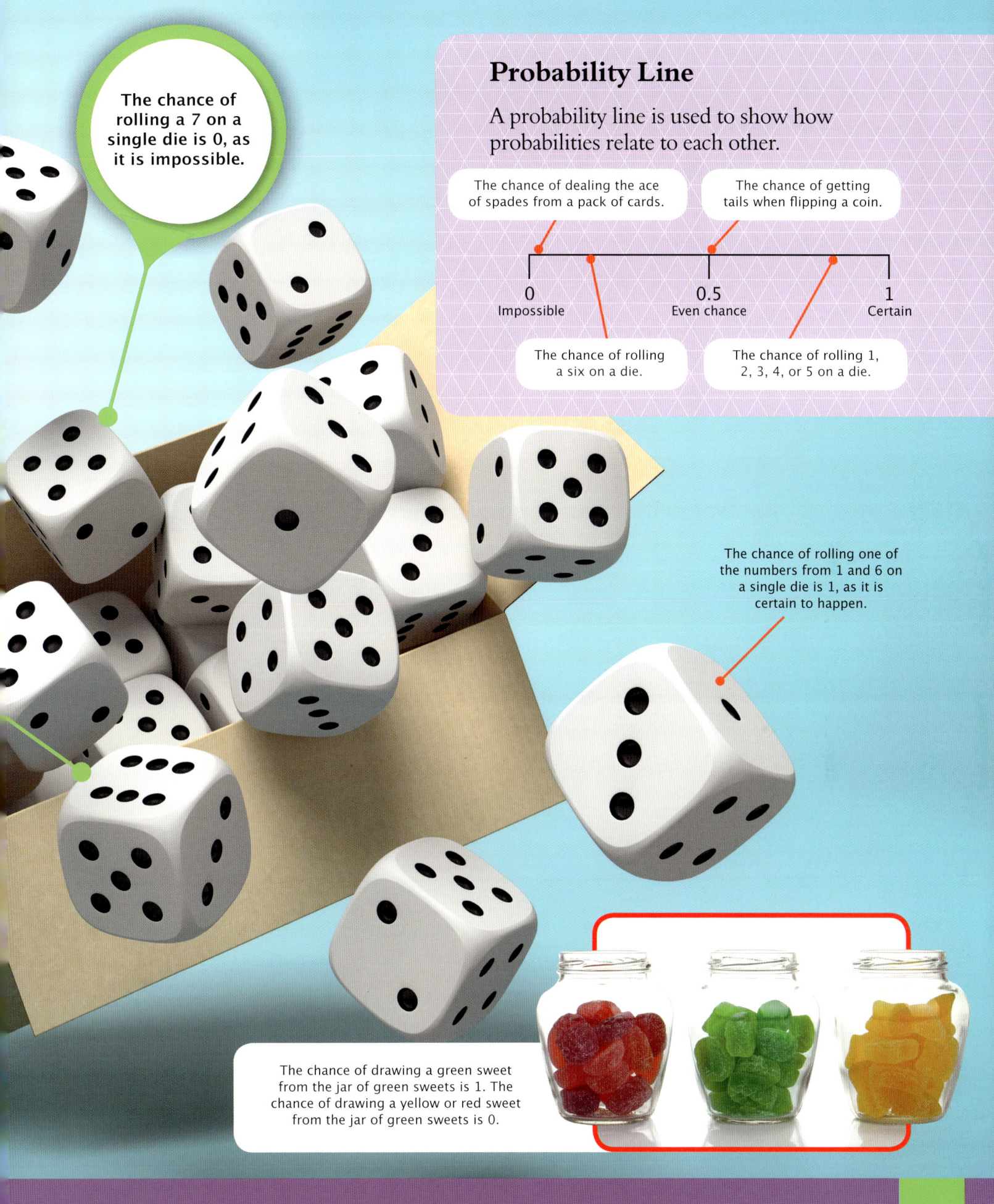

The chance of rolling a 7 on a single die is 0, as it is impossible.

Probability Line

A probability line is used to show how probabilities relate to each other.

The chance of dealing the ace of spades from a pack of cards.

The chance of getting tails when flipping a coin.

0 — Impossible
0.5 — Even chance
1 — Certain

The chance of rolling a six on a die.

The chance of rolling 1, 2, 3, 4, or 5 on a die.

The chance of rolling one of the numbers from 1 and 6 on a single die is 1, as it is certain to happen.

The chance of drawing a green sweet from the jar of green sweets is 1. The chance of drawing a yellow or red sweet from the jar of green sweets is 0.

81

Estimation

It's usually important to be precise in maths. But sometimes coming up with a good guess can be useful too. You might want to know how much wrapping paper to buy for a present, how thick to slice a birthday cake you're sharing with nine friends, or how much money the contents of your shopping basket will cost. You need to estimate.

Good Enough

You're not trying to find out the exact right answer when estimating, just one that's good enough for your purposes. For example, you might take a shopping basket containing six soft drinks costing 79p to a checkout till. The assistant asks you for £5.53 and you want to check that it's right. You round the drinks up to 80p each and quickly work out that six of them should cost less than £5. There's been a mistake and you need the assistant to recount.

> It would take a long time to count all the daisies in this field, but you could estimate the total from a sample.

Rounding

Rounding numbers up or down can make estimation easier. You might want to round 73 to the nearest 10, which would be 70. Or you might want to round 5.7523 to one decimal place, which would be 5.8. The digit 5 rounds up rather than down.

If something measured 82.5cm, you could round it up to 83cm.

MATHS FACT:
Rounding a Number

To 3 decimal places	67,382.592	To the nearest 10	67,380
To 2 decimal places	67,382.59	To the nearest 100	67,400
To 1 decimal place	67,382.6	To the nearest 1,000	67,000
To the nearest whole number	67,383	To the nearest 10,000	70,000

Find the total area of the field. Then measure out a small plot and count all the daisies inside it.

Divide the total area of the field by the area of the sample plot, then multiply this by the number of daisies you counted to produce your estimate.

You can improve your estimate by sampling another plot. Use the mean total of both plots to create the new estimate.

We often rely on calculators and apps, but it's possible to make mistakes without realizing it. If you get into the habit of estimating results, it's much easier to pick up on your mistakes.

DID YOU KNOW? When estimating, you can use the "approximately equals" symbol instead of the equals symbol. It looks like ≈ instead of =.

83

Chaos Theory

Maths typically deals with order. But a new branch of maths that emerged in the 20th century embraces unpredictability. Chaos theory looks at the way tiny changes in starting conditions can have a huge effect on end results. In the most famous example, it's said that a butterfly flapping its wings could cause a tornado hundreds of miles away.

Chaos in Life

It might sound like a bizarre idea, but chaos theory has practical uses. It was originally related to weather forecasting, but has since been applied to finance, artificial intelligence, population dynamics, and many other fields. Studying the small changes that make big differences is useful in lots of areas.

In 1972, the American mathematician Edward Lorenz delivered a talk called, "Does the flap of a butterfly's wings in Brazil set off a tornado in Texas?"

The Three Body Problem

The foundations of chaos theory were laid by French mathematician Henri Poincaré in the late 19th century in his work on the "three body problem." Mathematicians had been trying to find a way to predict the motion of three bodies held together by gravity, such as stars, planets, and moons. Poincaré argued that the bodies moved around each other in a way that was unpredictable and chaotic.

Three bodies bound together by gravity do not always move in simple, repeating patterns.

Lorenz described how a tiny change in atmospheric conditions, such as a butterfly flapping its wings, could eventually cause a major weather event elsewhere in the world.

DID YOU KNOW? Edward Lorenz originally wrote about the flap of a seagull's wings. It was only when the example was changed to a butterfly that the idea became famous.

Lorenz used early computers to model weather patterns. He found that changes as small as rounding from six decimal places to three decimal places, could have a dramatic effect on outcome. The butterfly was chosen as an example of something seemingly insignificant.

Ideas from chaos theory have been applied to many surprising areas. For example, they have been used to model the population of the Canadian lynx.

The idea captured the public imagination, and became known as "the butterfly effect."

HALL OF FAME: Edward Lorenz

Edward Lorenz was an American mathematician and meteorologist who was born in 1917 and died in 2008. He developed chaos theory when using computers to forecast weather, but its influence would go well beyond this field. It developed into a new branch of maths, and became one of the most important ideas of the twentieth century.

Chapter 5: Technology

The Abacus

We might think of the abacus as a toy used to teach children addition and subtraction, but it was a hugely important tool for centuries, and is still used in some parts of the world. Some traders in countries like China still use them, as do people with visual impairment.

The suan pan is a type of abacus used in China. It consists of beads on vertical rods divided into groups of two and five by a horizontal beam.

Pebbles and Slabs

The types of abacus that we use today feature rods with sliding beads. But early ones looked very different. The oldest surviving one is a marble slab dating from around 300 BCE, which is marked with horizontal lines. Pebbles were moved around it to make calculations.

The top two beads each have a value of five.

The bottom five beads each have a value of one.

The number six, for example, would be shown by moving one of the top beads down and one of the bottom beads up. 1 + 5 = 6.

MATHS FACT: Types of Abacus

Name	Features
Roman Abacus	Small pebbles are moved up and down vertical columns.
School Abacus	Plastic or wooden beads are moved horizontally on a wire.
Suan pan	Chinese abacus with separate columns of five beads and two beads.
Soroban	Japanese abacus with separate columns of four beads and one bead.

DID YOU KNOW? A "binary abacus" features rows of beads that slide into the "0" and "1" values of the binary system. It's used to teach students about computers.

The Soroban

The soroban is a Japanese abacus that developed from the suan pan. They are still popular in Japanese schools, and students compete to see who can use them the fastest in annual soroban championships.

The top bead has a value of five.

The four bottom beads have a value of one.

The Cranmer Abacus was developed for blind and partially-sighted people. Soft fabric or rubber behind the beads helps to keep them in place.

87

The Computer

In 1837, English mathematician Charles Babbage designed the first general purpose counting machine, called the "Analytical Engine." Another mathematician called Ada Lovelace wrote a sequence of instructions to program it. Although both Babbage and Lovelace died before the Analytical Engine was built, they'd laid the groundwork for an invention that would change the world—the computer.

Microchips

The first electronic computers were big enough to fill entire rooms. The invention of microchips in the 1950s meant computers could get smaller and increase in processing power. The home computer emerged in the 1970s, and since then, their power has developed at a staggering rate. We are now surrounded by high-tech gadgets that would have been unthinkable to previous generations.

The development of microchips led to the introduction of home computers in the 1970s and 1980s. Microchips are small pieces of silicon with electronic circuits on, and they've been called one of the most important inventions in the history of humankind.

ENIAC, the Electronic Numerical Integrator and Computer, was built by the US during World War II. It took days to rewire the machine for each new problem.

Early personal computers were sold as a kit that users had to put together themselves. The release of "pre-assembled" computers in the late 1970s meant that they could be sold to a wider audience.

HALL OF FAME: Charles Babbage

Charles Babbage was an English mathematician and inventor who was born in 1791 and died in 1871. In the 1820s, he invented a calculating machine called the "difference engine." He followed it in the 1830s with plans for the "analytical engine," which could follow instructions from punched cards, and is seen as the forerunner of the modern computer.

Punch Cards

Punch cards were used to input data into early computers. A special machine was used to cut holes into stiff paper cards. They were stacked in decks and had to be kept in the right order.

Holes were made in cards. The cards were then fed into a reader connected to a computer, which converted the sequence of holes into information.

Home computers were originally used for things like word-processing and managing money, but they soon became popular for playing video games.

The principle that computer processing power doubles every two years is known as "Moore's Law," after engineer Gordon Moore.

DID YOU KNOW? The Apple II was one of the first popular home computers. It launched in 1977 at a price of $1,298, equivalent to over $5,500 now.

Barcodes

Barcodes are a good example of how maths is everywhere, sometimes in ways we don't notice. Those tiny rectangles of stripes that appear on the things we buy represent the digits from 0 to 9. Each barcode creates a unique number that can be read by a scanner.

> Barcodes are clearer than numbers. When reading numbers, it's easy to mistake a 1 for a 7 or a 3 for an 8.

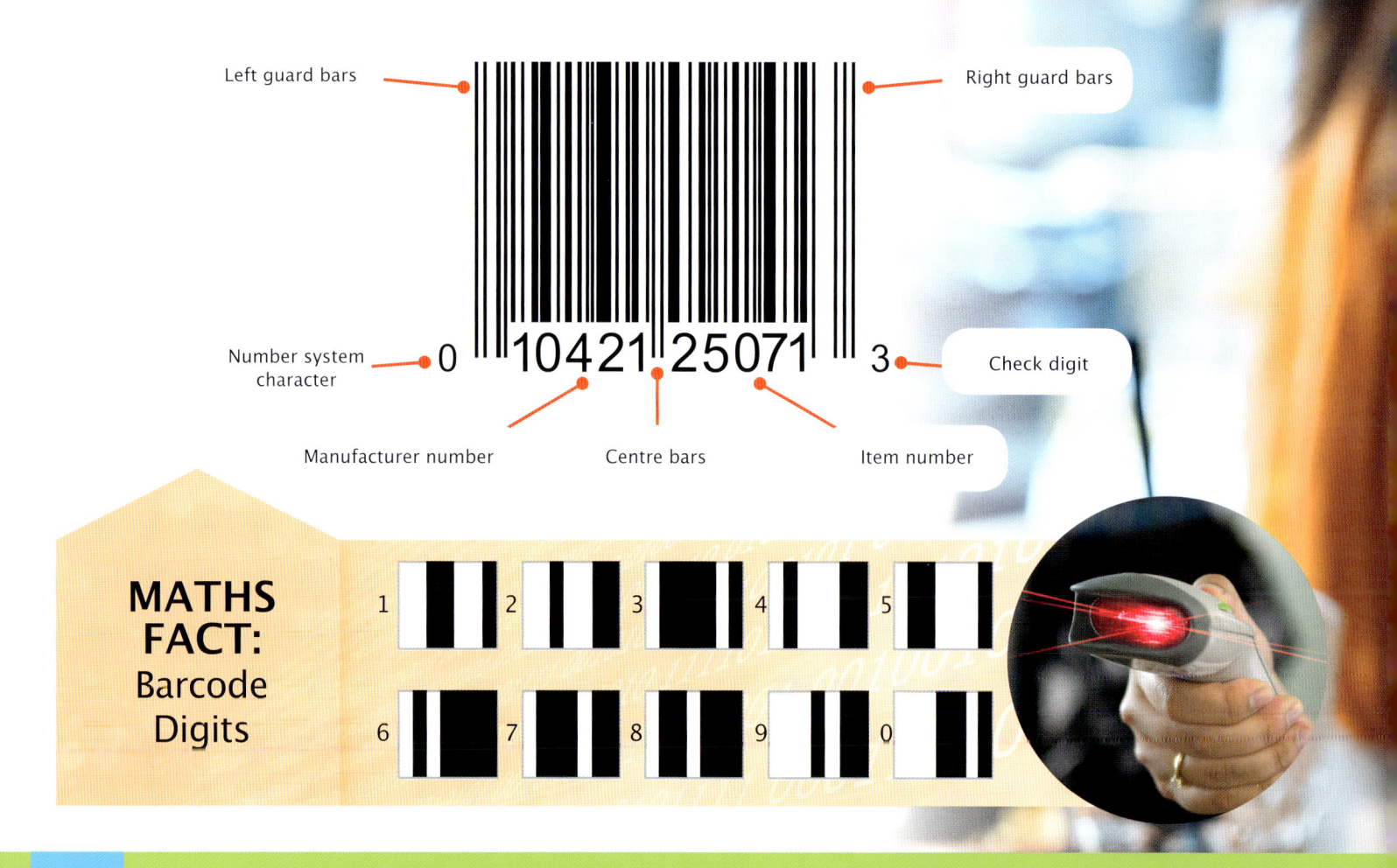

Cutting Down Queues

An American inventor called Joe Woodland came up with the idea of barcodes in 1949, after he had heard that supermarket managers needed a way to get customers through their stores quicker so they could cut down on queues. It wasn't until 1974, however, that barcodes were introduced in shops.

Left guard bars · Right guard bars · Number system character · 0 10421 25071 3 · Check digit · Manufacturer number · Centre bars · Item number

MATHS FACT: Barcode Digits

1 2 3 4 5
6 7 8 9 0

90

The check digit is used to make sure a barcode has scanned or been inputted properly. It is calculated using all the other digits in the code.

Barcodes can still be read upside down, unlike numbers.

This type of barcode is known as a UPC, or Universal Product Code. It consists of twelve digits that are unique to each item.

When a barcode is scanned, the product is automatically removed from the shop's inventory. This allows shops to keep track of stock levels.

QR Codes

A QR, or "quick response," code is a type of barcode consisting of squares on a white background. It was devised in Japan in 1994 and became popular because it can store more data than a standard UPC.

QR codes can be scanned by smartphones. They are used to give information such as web addresses.

DID YOU KNOW? The first item to be scanned at a checkout was a pack of chewing gum.

Secret Codes

For centuries, maths has been used to create codes and keep secrets. Messages can be written in code by shifting letters along in the alphabet, plotting them on grids, and even giving page references to a particular book. The making and breaking of codes has played a part in some of the most important moments in history, such as World War II.

Cracking the Code

Some secret codes are easy to generate. You could substitute each letter with a number, a symbol, or a different letter. But codes like this can be broken. The most commonly used letters in your code are likely to stand for the most commonly used letters in your language. For example, if your code uses H the most, it probably stands for E, the most common letter in English. Codebreakers can use this principle to work through your entire message.

Can maths save lives? The team of mathematicians who cracked the Enigma code are thought to have shortened World War II.

The German military were using the "Enigma machine" to encrypt messages. There were millions of solutions to every piece of coded text, and the device's settings changed every night. The code seemed unbreakable.

HALL OF FAME: Alan Turing

Alan Turing was a British mathematician who was born in 1912 and died in 1954. His codebreaking work at Bletchley Park during World War II helped shorten the war, and save the lives of millions, but it had to remain secret for many years afterward. Turing was also a hugely important figure in the development of computer science and artificial intelligence.

DID YOU KNOW? Kryptos is a sculpture located outside the headquarters of the CIA in Langley, USA. It features four coded messages, three of which have been solved, and one that never has.

Nuclear Codes

Some secret codes could end life as we know it. The "gold codes" are given to the President of the United States on a card. They launch nuclear missiles that could destroy entire cities.

Every day, the president of the USA is given a card containing several fake nuclear codes and one real one. The president knows which is genuine from its location on the card.

If the Allied mathematicians could read the secret messages, they could find out when the Nazis were planning to attack Britain.

Julius Caesar used a system of replacing each letter with the one three places along in the alphabet, so A becomes D, and so on. Shifting letters along by a fixed number of places is now known as the "Caesar Cipher."

Alan Turing developed a device called "the Bombe" which used probability to discount millions of unlikely solutions. The other mathematicians could then work on the ones that were left.

93

Security

As our lives have moved online, so has criminal activity. Cyber criminals try to exploit vulnerabilities in security to steal passwords, data, and credit card details. They cost the world trillions of dollars every year, and their methods are getting more sophisticated all the time.

Encryption is used to protect your data from cyber criminals. It uses an algorithm to scramble data and a "key" so that whoever is receiving the data can unscramble it.

Hacking and Phishing

Cyber criminals can breach security through methods such as hacking and phishing. Hacking is accessing private details through things like guessing hundreds of passwords until you get the right one. Phishing is pretending to be a trustworthy source to get people to give up the data themselves. For example, a phisher could send out an email pretending to be from a bank and asking people to enter their details.

Keep It Locked

Numerical codes are used to protect everything from your bike to your cash card. There are 10,000 possible four-digit codes, so it would take thieves a long time to find the right one by trial and error.

Never use 1234 or 1111 as your code. And avoid things that could be found out like your birthday. Try using a different memorable date instead.

DID YOU KNOW? Lots of people use the name of their favourite sports team as a password. Avoid this, as it's too easy for hackers to guess.

The original information is known as "plaintext," and the scrambled information is known as "ciphertext."

Cyber criminals use "brute force attacks" to guess passwords and keys. They work through all possible combinations until they get the right one.

Choosing a long password can protect against brute force attacks, as there are many more possibilities for the hacker to go through.

Stay safe online! Never give out information such as your name and address without permission from a parent or guardian.

MATHS FACT:
The Ten Most Popular Passwords

123456	12345678
123456789	abc123
qwerty	1234567
password	password1
111111	12345

Traffic

As populations increase, roads get busier, and controlling the flow of traffic becomes more difficult. But we can turn to maths for help. Through mathematical models of traffic, planners can work out things like how to schedule public transport, how to operate traffic signals, and where to build new roads.

Smart Motorways

Examining the movement of traffic can produce some surprising results. For example, it's been found that lowering speed limits can reduce congestion and help with traffic flow, letting people get to their destinations faster. "Smart motorways" have electronic signs that can change the speed limit and keep a smooth flow of traffic.

People often complain that they wait ages for a bus and then two come at once. But transport planners aren't doing it deliberately to annoy everyone. In fact, it makes mathematical sense.

Imagine two buses are travelling around the same route. If the one in front suffers a minor delay, or has to stop to let a big group of passengers on, the one behind will catch up.

The slight delay slows the first bus down, meaning more passengers will gather at the upcoming stops, and it will take longer to get them on. Meanwhile, the second bus gets closer, and has fewer passengers to pick up at each stop. Eventually the two buses bunch together.

MATHS FACT: Modelling a Rush Hour Queue

Time	Number of cars arriving at traffic lights	Number of cars going through on green light	Number of cars in queue
8:00	9	9	0
8:01	10	10	0
8:02	11	10	1
8:03	12	10	3
8:04	13	10	6

DID YOU KNOW? A 2019 study estimated that British drivers will spend an average of eight months of their lives stuck in traffic jams.

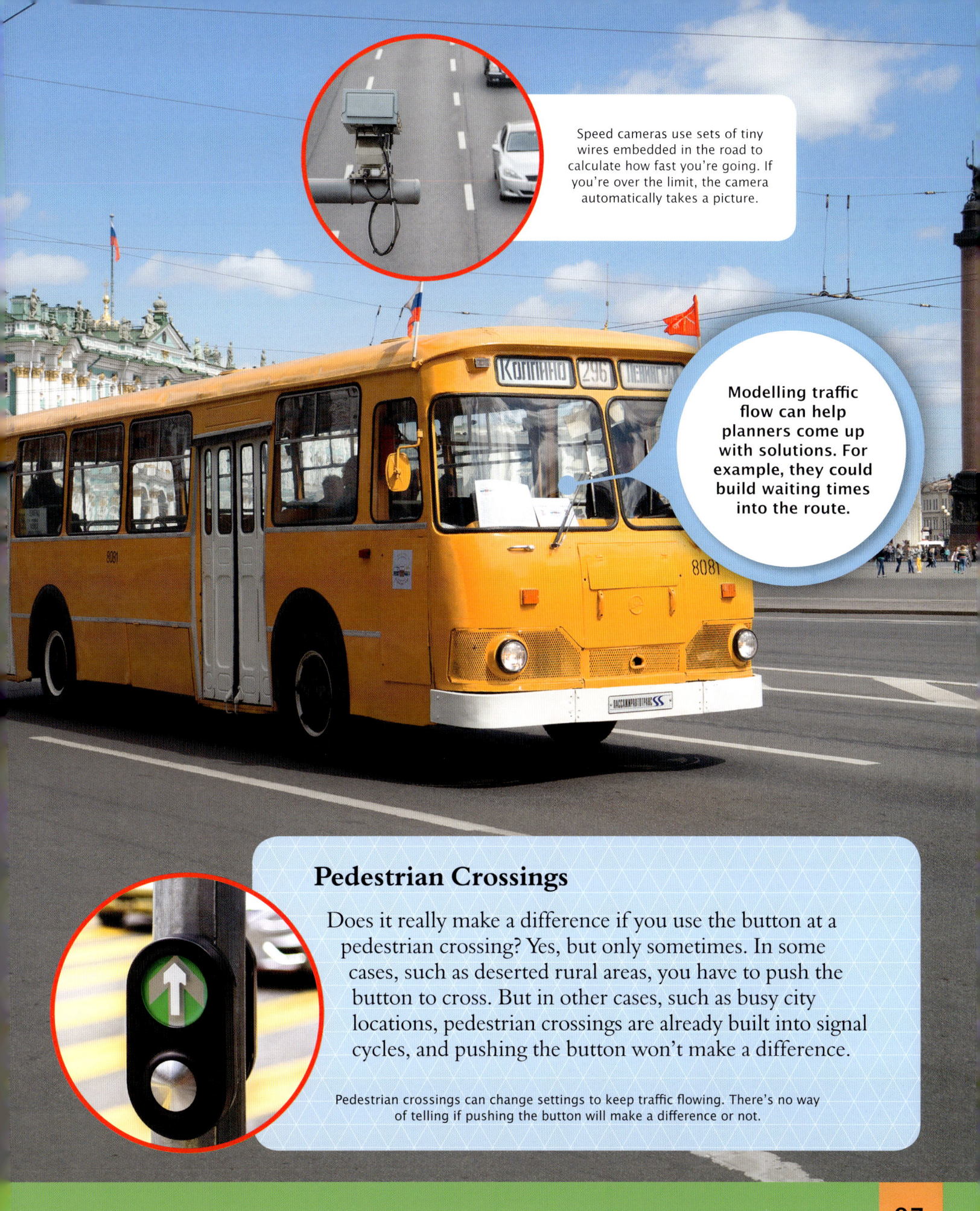

Speed cameras use sets of tiny wires embedded in the road to calculate how fast you're going. If you're over the limit, the camera automatically takes a picture.

Modelling traffic flow can help planners come up with solutions. For example, they could build waiting times into the route.

Pedestrian Crossings

Does it really make a difference if you use the button at a pedestrian crossing? Yes, but only sometimes. In some cases, such as deserted rural areas, you have to push the button to cross. But in other cases, such as busy city locations, pedestrian crossings are already built into signal cycles, and pushing the button won't make a difference.

Pedestrian crossings can change settings to keep traffic flowing. There's no way of telling if pushing the button will make a difference or not.

97

Buildings

Mathematical knowledge has always been used in building design. The Roman architect Vitruvius, who lived in the first century BCE, stressed the need for symmetry and perfect proportion. His ideas were rediscovered in the 14th and 15th centuries and had a huge influence on the era. Maths has also shaped the way buildings are decorated, as with the tessellating patterns of Islamic architecture.

Geodesic domes look spherical, but are actually made from triangles. The structure is strong, and uses much less material than conventional buildings.

Computer-Aided Design

Today, architects and engineers use computer-aided design to create tall skyscrapers, long bridges, and giant shopping centres. Their mathematical knowledge helps them choose strong structures, make the best use of materials, and produce buildings that are energy-efficient.

Triangles are sturdy shapes. Because the domes are made from them, they can withstand wind, snow, and even earthquakes.

Arches

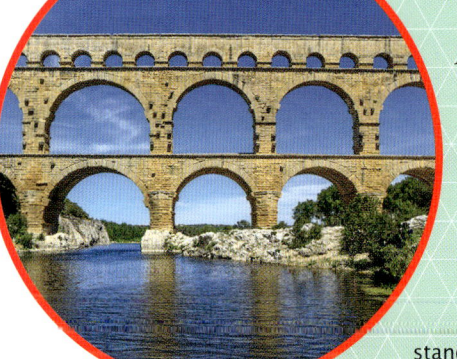

Arches are robust shapes that have been used in architecture for centuries. They are good at holding weight, and are often used for doorways, windows, and bridges.

This Roman aqueduct in France is still standing almost 2,000 years after it was built.

The structure gets its name from a geodesic, the shortest line between any two points on a curved surface.

DID YOU KNOW? From 1975 to 2010 there was a geodesic dome at the South Pole. It was used as a scientific research station.

30 St Mary Axe, London, has been given the nickname "the Gherkin" because of its unusual shape. The shape can be created by revolving a curve around an axis, and is an example of a "solid of revolution."

Geodesic domes have been used for sports arenas, greenhouses, and theatres. This one in Montreal, Canada, houses a museum.

MATHS FACT: Shapes in Architecture

Shape	Example
Triangle	Flatiron Building, New York, USA
Pentagon	Headquarters of the Department of Defense in Virginia, USA
Octagon	Florence Baptistery, Italy
Decahedron	Momine Khatun Mausoleum, Azerbaijan

99

Algorithms

An algorithm is a series of step-by-step instructions to solve a problem. Computers use algorithms, so we associate the word with technology. But it can also refer to any list of rules we would use in real life, like a recipe to bake a cake, or a set of directions to the local shops. They are simple steps that need to be followed to get a result.

Addition Algorithm

Calculations can be written as simple sets of instructions. For example, if we want to add two-digit numbers together we might follow this algorithm: Step 1, add the tens. Step 2, add the ones. Step 3, add the results of Step 1 and Step 2. So if we wanted to add 42 and 83, we'd follow the instructions like this:

Step 1 $40 + 80 = 120$
Step 2 $2 + 3 = 5$
Step 3 $120 + 5 = 125$

If you follow a set of instructions for a construction toy, you are using an algorithm. The process is broken down step by step to make sure you perform the actions in the right order.

Robotic toys are used to teach algorithms. Users have to plan a series of step-by-step instructions and input them to make the robots perform simple tasks.

HALL OF FAME: Ada Lovelace

Ada Lovelace was born in London in 1815 and died in 1852. She has been called "the world's first computer programmer" for her work on Charles Babbage's analytical engine. She devised an algorithm that would make the machine generate a sequence of numbers. The algorithm was never tested in her lifetime, but its importance has now been acknowledged.

DID YOU KNOW? Algorithms have been found on ancient Babylonian clay tablets dating from around 1800–1600 BCE.

Flowcharts

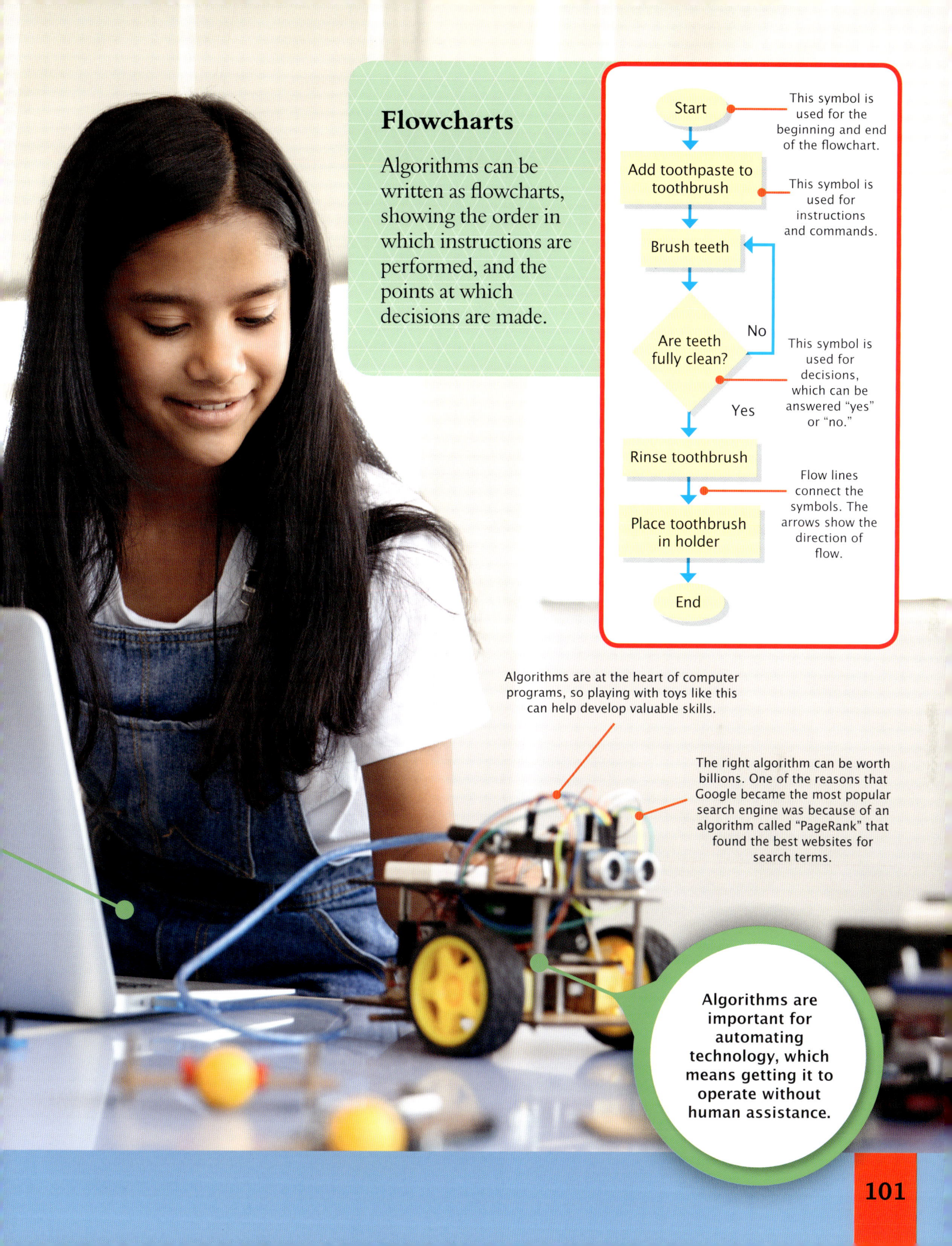

Algorithms can be written as flowcharts, showing the order in which instructions are performed, and the points at which decisions are made.

Start — This symbol is used for the beginning and end of the flowchart.

Add toothpaste to toothbrush — This symbol is used for instructions and commands.

Brush teeth

Are teeth fully clean? — This symbol is used for decisions, which can be answered "yes" or "no."
- No → Brush teeth
- Yes ↓

Rinse toothbrush

Place toothbrush in holder — Flow lines connect the symbols. The arrows show the direction of flow.

End

Algorithms are at the heart of computer programs, so playing with toys like this can help develop valuable skills.

The right algorithm can be worth billions. One of the reasons that Google became the most popular search engine was because of an algorithm called "PageRank" that found the best websites for search terms.

Algorithms are important for automating technology, which means getting it to operate without human assistance.

101

Space Travel

Humans first travelled into space in the latter half of the twentieth century. The satellite Sputnik 1 was launched in 1957, and Yuri Gagarin became the first person to orbit the Earth in 1961. These milestones sparked the "space race" between the Soviet Union and the USA. Maths was crucial in designing and building spacecraft and planning their trajectories.

Celestial Mechanics

"Celestial mechanics" studies the motion of objects in space. It uses the laws first described by Isaac Newton in the 17th century. Over 300 years after he was born, Newton's work was used to send humans into space. During the Apollo 8 mission, astronaut Bill Anders said, "I think Isaac Newton is doing most of the driving now."

The Apollo program was run by NASA, the National Aeronautics and Space Administration, between 1961 and 1972.

Gravity assist was used by the Voyager space probes launched by NASA in 1977.

Gravity Assist

Mathematical calculations can be used to plan space flights in ingenious ways. A spacecraft can use the gravity of a planet or moon to speed up, slow down, or change direction. This is known as "gravity assist."

HALL OF FAME: Katherine Johnson

Katherine Johnson was an American mathematician who was born in 1918 and died in 2020. She calculated the flight paths of many spacecraft while working at NASA. In the early 1960s, she worked out paths for NASA's first crewed spaceflights, and in 1969, she was part of the team behind the successful Apollo 11 mission.

The Apollo 11 mission landed the first humans on the moon on July 20, 1969.

Before it became associated with technology, the word "computer" was used to refer to people who carried out mathematical calculations. The human computers who worked at NASA, supervised by Dorothy Vaughan, have now been recognized for their contribution to the space race.

The Apollo Guidance Computer had a tiny amount of memory and processing power compared to modern technology. Your phone is thousands of times more powerful than the computer that took humans to the moon.

Mathematicians used Isaac Newton's laws of motion to plot the paths of spacecraft. Could Newton have predicted how far his ideas would take humankind?

DID YOU KNOW? The maths developed for the Apollo program is now used to manage air traffic.

Networks

We encounter many networks in our daily lives. The internet is a network that links physical devices such as phones and computers. Social networks link our friends and acquaintances. And transport networks such as bus and train routes link physical locations.

Nodes and Edges

Mathematicians can model all these different types of network in the same way. The things that are connected to each other are called "nodes," the links between them are called "edges," and the number of edges meeting at a node is called its "degree." This field of maths is known as "graph theory."

Swiss mathematician Leonhard Euler came up with a solution to a mathematical puzzle that shaped the way we see networks.

The Prussian city of Königsberg, now in Russia and known as Kaliningrad, had seven bridges. They connected both sides of the city with the two islands in the middle of the River Pregel. The locals wondered if it were possible to visit each part of the city by crossing each bridge just once.

Eulerian Paths

The seven bridges problem can be reduced to a diagram. The distances and shapes aren't relevant to the puzzle, just the number of nodes and the number of connections between them.

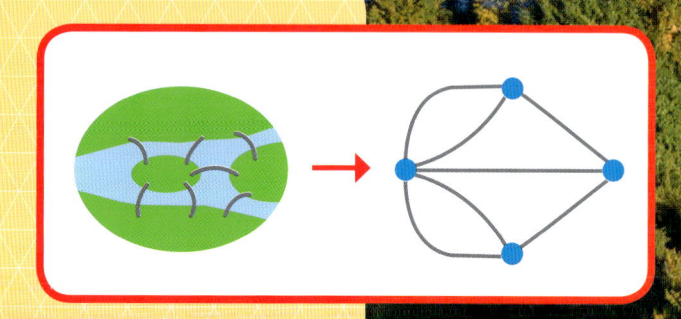

If a path can reach every node while passing through each edge just once, it's known as a "Eulerian path."

DID YOU KNOW? Euler's work is an example of "proof by contradiction." If a statement leads to a conclusion which cannot be true, then it means the original statement is incorrect. Therefore the opposite of the original statement must be true.

Euler proved that a route through the city that crossed each bridge just once was impossible.

Social networks can be shown through diagrams like the one of Königsberg. The nodes represent people rather than land masses, and the connections show friendships rather than bridges.

Euler reasoned that someone arriving on an area of land would have to leave by a different bridge, so the bridges would have to exist in pairs. As all four areas were connected by an odd rather than an even number of bridges, it wasn't possible to go through the city passing over each bridge just once.

HALL OF FAME: Leonhard Euler

Leonhard Euler was born in Switzerland in 1707 and died in 1783. He made huge contributions to many fields of maths, including calculus, geometry, and trigonometry. The irrational number e, which is approximately equal to 2.718, is called "Euler's number" after him. He lost his sight toward the end of his life, but kept up his remarkable work rate.

Chapter 6: Maths in Life

Puzzles

Some maths is done just for fun. "Recreational maths" is the name given to puzzles and games inspired by different areas of maths. It covers everything from plastic toys to memes to sudokus in newspapers. The best examples cross over to a wide audience who might not see themselves as interested in maths.

Crazes

Puzzles can sometimes get so popular that they become international crazes. In the 1980s, over 200 million Rubik's cubes were sold. In the early 2000s, a sudoku fad spread from Japan to the rest of the world, and sudoku contests were even televised in some countries. In our current era, tricky maths puzzles often go viral on social media and get millions of views.

Sudoku developed from number puzzles based on magic squares. Parts of the magic square were left blank, and players had to calculate the missing numbers.

Magic Squares

Magic squares date back to ancient China, and can be found in early mathematical writings in India, Europe, and the Middle East. They even appear in famous works of art, such as Albrecht Dürer's 1514 engraving *Melencolia I*.

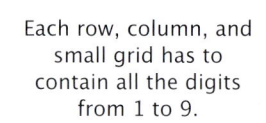

The total of each row, column, and main diagonal are the same on a magic square. In this square, from a church in Barcelona, the numbers always add up to 33, a reference to the age of Christ when he died.

Each row, column, and small grid has to contain all the digits from 1 to 9.

DID YOU KNOW? In 2018, the world's largest multi-sudoku puzzle was created in Japan. It consisted of 280 overlapping grids.

HALL OF FAME: Lewis Carroll

Charles Lutwidge Dodgson, who wrote under the name Lewis Carroll, was an English mathematician who was born in 1832 and died in 1898. As well as working in the fields of geometry and algebra, he devised hundreds of puzzles and even came up with a board game called "The Game of Logic," which was used to explain the principles of mathematical logic. He is best remembered as the author of *Alice's Adventures in Wonderland*.

Sudoku players have to complete all the numbers on the grid. The puzzle setter will often give each grid a difficulty level.

The smallest number of clues that a sudoku grid can have and still be solvable is 17.

How many blocks are needed to complete a full cube? This maths puzzle has been shared by millions online. Can you work out the answer?

Answer: Read the question carefully and you'll see that 55 blocks are needed. You could fill the gaps with 30 blocks, but that wouldn't make it a cube!

107

Music

Maths and music might seem to be very different worlds. One is rational and scientific while the other is artistic and creative. Yet they are deeply linked. There are mathematical relationships between the sounds that appeal to us. And classical composers and modern musicians have written music inspired by maths.

Pythagoras

Some of the earliest ideas about maths and music are attributed to the ancient Greek philosopher Pythagoras. He's said to have discovered that halving the length of a string will produce the same note, one octave higher. And that doubling the length of a string will produce the same note an octave lower.

When you pluck a guitar string, it vibrates and sends sound waves through the air.

Different notes have different wavelengths.

DID YOU KNOW? Pythagoras and his followers thought the planets made sounds as they moved, but humans couldn't hear them. This was known as the "music of the spheres."

Dance

Dance has strong links to maths too. Different mathematical ratios lie behind the rhythms of waltzes, polkas, and sambas. And many dances are based on reflectional and rotational symmetry.

A waltz is danced to a $\frac{3}{4}$ time signature, which has three beats to each bar. Dancers count from one to three over and over again as they're learning a waltz.

Notes that sound good together have simple ratios in wavelength. For example, if two notes are an octave apart, one has exactly half the wavelength of the other. We say they are in "harmony."

Computer software can make you sing in tune. Auto-Tune was invented in the 1990s, and uses complex maths to correct the pitch of vocals. It has become a common feature of modern pop.

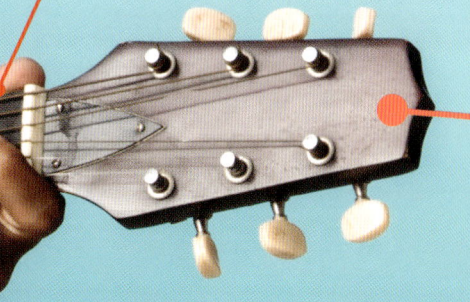

A note will also sound good alongside one with a wavelength one-and-a-half times as long. Notes that don't sound good together have no simple ratio between their wavelengths.

MATHS FACT:
Simple Time Signatures

Notation	Name	Common Uses
$\frac{2}{4}$	Duple	Polkas and Marches
$\frac{3}{4}$	Triple	Waltzes and Minuets
$\frac{4}{4}$	Quadruple	Rock and Pop

109

Searching

A mathematical paper published over 250 years ago still influences things like how doctors test for diseases and how banks decide who to lend money to. It outlined what is known as "Bayes' theorem," and one of the most important ways we use it is to search for missing things.

Updating Probability

Bayes' theorem is a formula for working out probability that allows us to change our predictions as we go along. Probabilities are updated as new data is found, helping us to decide where to focus our attention. It can be used to find everything from lost pets to missing aircraft.

If someone is lost at sea, information such as where they were last seen and where they were heading, as well as things like tides, wind, and currents, can be combined to create a map showing where they are most likely to be.

Bayes' ideas have influenced recommendation filters on streaming sites. Our viewing choices are used to update predictions about what we might want next.

HALL OF FAME: Thomas Bayes

Thomas Bayes was an English minister and mathematician who was born around 1701 and died in 1761. The theorem that we remember him for was never published in his lifetime. It was presented to the Royal Society and brought into print shortly after he died. Bayes could hardly have guessed how much of our lives all these years later would be influenced by his ideas.

DID YOU KNOW? The wreckage of the U.S. Navy's submarine *Scorpion* was found using Bayes' theorem in 1968.

Rescue ships will search areas in order of the probability that the missing person is there.

Filtering Emails

Bayes' theorem can be used to build "spam filters" that keep unwanted emails away from our inboxes. It can update the chances that emails are spam based on the ones we read and the ones we delete.

Phrases like "best price" or punctuation like $$$ mean an email has a high probability of being unwanted.

Software based on Bayes' theorem uses new data to constantly update the map and guide rescue crews.

Bayes' theorem can be used to weigh the cost of a search against the probability of it being successful.

Game Theory

Game theory is a branch of maths that deals with decision-making. It regards real-life situations as games with winners and losers. It looks at the strategies people can use to get the best outcomes for themselves and beat their opponents. It has been a hugely influential area of maths since it was developed almost a hundred years ago.

> The prisoners' dilemma is a famous puzzle that's used as an example of game theory.

Beating your Competitors

There are many imaginary situations which have been invented to demonstrate game theory, such as the "prisoner's dilemma." But it can be used to everyday life too. It is especially useful in business, where companies try and work out what their competitors are going to do. Game theory can help them decide whether to do things like advertise or cut prices.

Imagine two prisoners have been suspected of robbery and placed in separate cells. They are both urged to confess without knowing what the other has said.

1. If both confess, they both go to jail for five years.
2. If neither confesses, they both go to jail for one year.
3. If one of them confesses and the other doesn't, the first prisoner is set free, while the other goes to jail for 20 years.

A company might use a pay-off matrix to decide whether to cut the price of a product. If they cut their price and their rival doesn't, they'll sell more. But if they cut their price and their rival does too, they'll both sell the same amount, but for less money.

112

HALL OF FAME: John von Neumann

John von Neumann was a mathematician who was born in Hungary in 1903 and died in the US in 1957. He developed game theory to address problems in economics. He also made major contributions to geometry, topology, and physics, and was one of the founders of modern computing.

Each prisoner might run through their options and decide it's better to confess. But the best thing for both of them overall would be if they stayed silent.

Pay-off Matrix

A pay-off matrix helps people look at all their options and decide which is best.

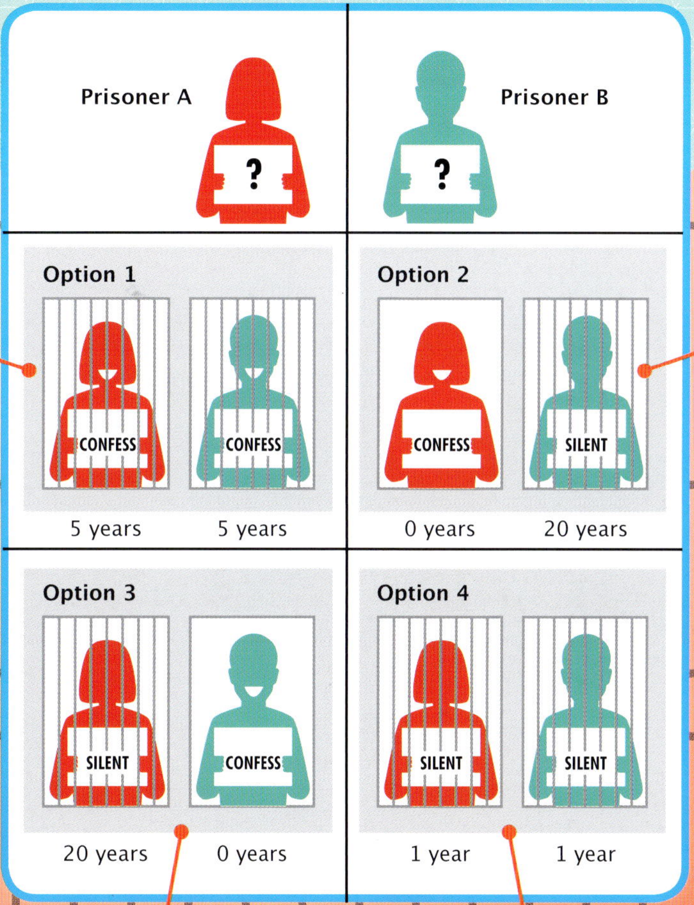

Prisoner A / **Prisoner B**

Option 1: CONFESS / CONFESS — 5 years / 5 years

Option 2: CONFESS / SILENT — 0 years / 20 years

Option 3: SILENT / CONFESS — 20 years / 0 years

Option 4: SILENT / SILENT — 1 year / 1 year

If both prisoners confess, they'll both go to jail for five years.

If prisoner A confesses and prisoner B stays silent, prisoner A goes free, while prisoner B goes to jail for 20 years.

If prisoner B confesses and prisoner A stays silent, prisoner B goes free, while prisoner A goes to jail for 20 years.

If both prisoners stay silent, they both go to jail for one year.

DID YOU KNOW? Some people use game theory to help with tricky situations such as negotiating prices and asking for a pay rise.

113

Art

Maths impacted many eras of art. The introduction of perspective transformed art in the 15th century. Before then, the size of objects in paintings related to things like their importance, rather than their distance from each other. Perspective allowed artists to show depth and changed the way people and objects were arranged.

Inspired by Maths

Other aspects of maths have influenced different art periods. Symmetry and tessellation were hallmarks of traditional Islamic art. De Stijl, the Dutch art movement of the early 20th century, embraced geometric shapes but avoided symmetry. And modern computer art has taken inspiration from fractals.

If you wanted to draw or paint this scene, you could start with guidelines to make sure you get the perspective right. You could include a horizon line, orthogonal lines, and a vanishing point.

The columns, rows, and diagonals on this magic square all add up to 34. The two numbers in the middle on the bottom also give the date of the engraving, 1514.

This is called a "truncated triangular trapezohedron." It is now called "Dürer's Solid" because of this engraving.

Melencolia I

The 1514 engraving "Melencolia I" by the German artist Albrecht Dürer contains many references to geometry and maths. It features a compass, sphere, an unusual solid, and a magic square.

The horizon line is where the land meets the sky.

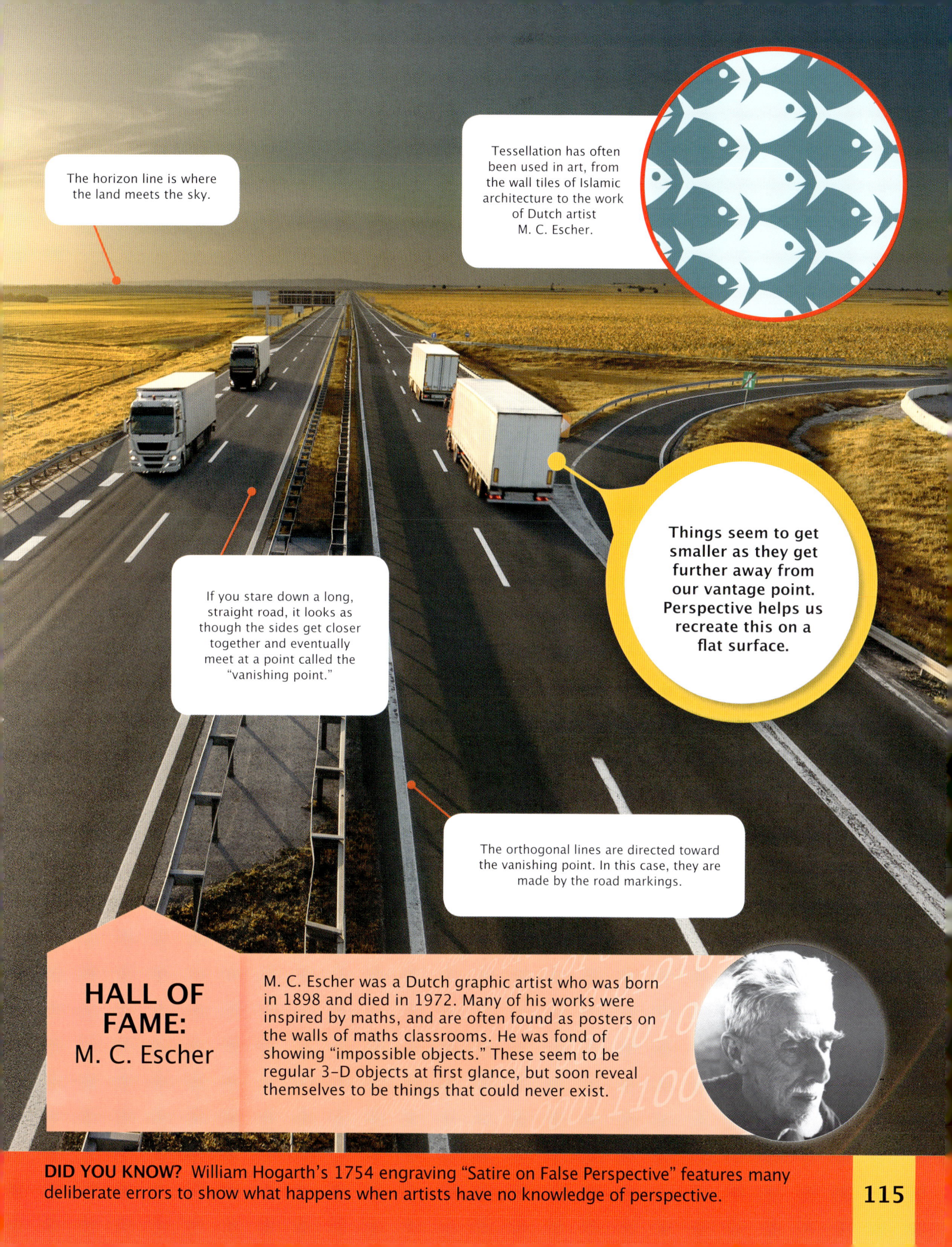

Tessellation has often been used in art, from the wall tiles of Islamic architecture to the work of Dutch artist M. C. Escher.

If you stare down a long, straight road, it looks as though the sides get closer together and eventually meet at a point called the "vanishing point."

Things seem to get smaller as they get further away from our vantage point. Perspective helps us recreate this on a flat surface.

The orthogonal lines are directed toward the vanishing point. In this case, they are made by the road markings.

HALL OF FAME: M. C. Escher

M. C. Escher was a Dutch graphic artist who was born in 1898 and died in 1972. Many of his works were inspired by maths, and are often found as posters on the walls of maths classrooms. He was fond of showing "impossible objects." These seem to be regular 3-D objects at first glance, but soon reveal themselves to be things that could never exist.

DID YOU KNOW? William Hogarth's 1754 engraving "Satire on False Perspective" features many deliberate errors to show what happens when artists have no knowledge of perspective.

115

Diseases

In a time of crisis, maths can help. When there's an outbreak of a disease, mathematical models let us track how fast it's spreading, and work out what difference things like face masks and social distancing will make. The models allow countries to work out what precautions they need to take to make sure their health systems can cope.

Pandemics

In the year 2020, the COVID-19 pandemic turned maths into headline news. Graphs of infections were widely shared and terms such as "reproductive number" and "flattening the curve" became part of everyday conversation. It was the latest in a line of pandemics that included an influenza outbreak in 1968 and swine flu in 2009.

The basic reproductive number, or R0, of a disease is the average number of people that an infected person will go on to infect.

Flattening the Curve

When a disease breaks out, governments try to slow the spread so that there are enough doctors, nurses, and hospital beds to take care of all the infected people who need them. Measures such as closing shops and schools can make sure healthcare systems don't get overloaded. This is known as "flattening the curve."

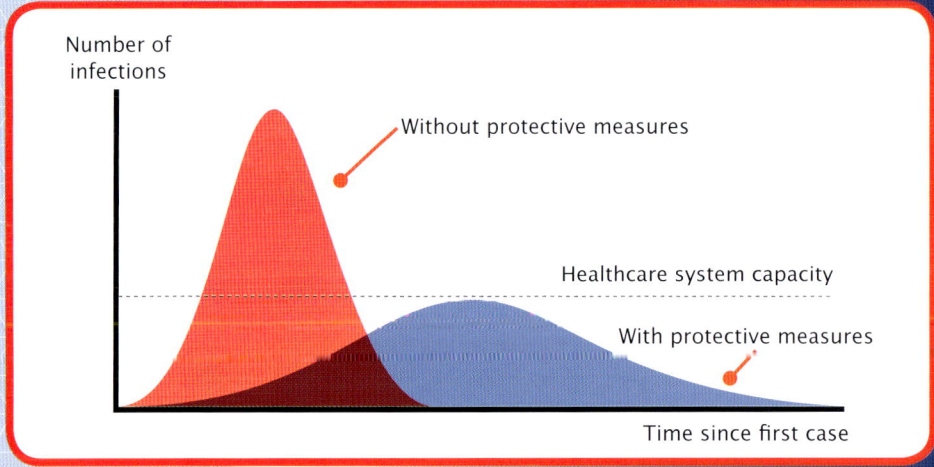

DID YOU KNOW? The R0 number for measles is very high, so it can have explosive outbreaks.

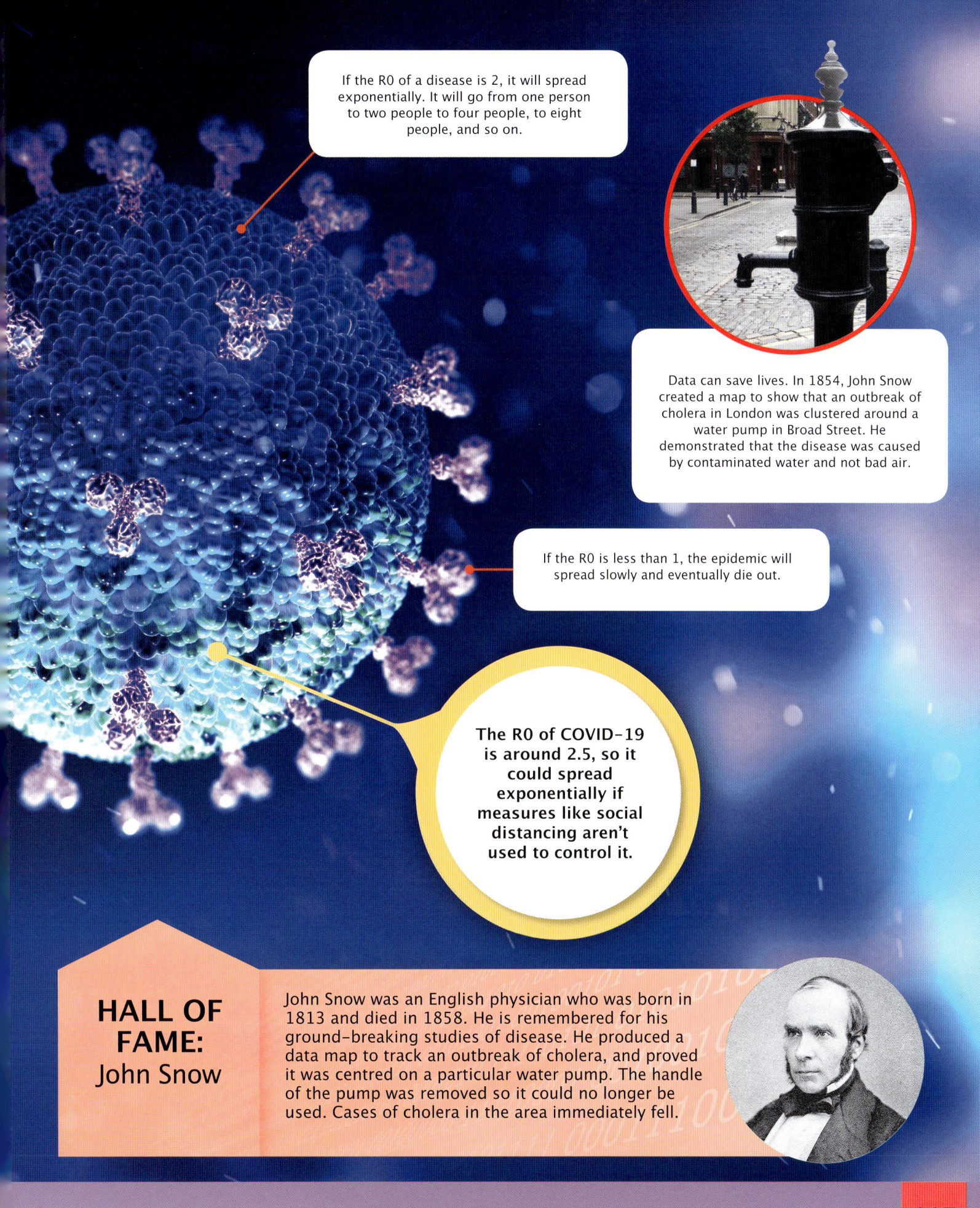

If the R0 of a disease is 2, it will spread exponentially. It will go from one person to two people to four people, to eight people, and so on.

Data can save lives. In 1854, John Snow created a map to show that an outbreak of cholera in London was clustered around a water pump in Broad Street. He demonstrated that the disease was caused by contaminated water and not bad air.

If the R0 is less than 1, the epidemic will spread slowly and eventually die out.

The R0 of COVID-19 is around 2.5, so it could spread exponentially if measures like social distancing aren't used to control it.

HALL OF FAME: John Snow

John Snow was an English physician who was born in 1813 and died in 1858. He is remembered for his ground-breaking studies of disease. He produced a data map to track an outbreak of cholera, and proved it was centred on a particular water pump. The handle of the pump was removed so it could no longer be used. Cases of cholera in the area immediately fell.

Sequences

A sequence is a list of numbers in order, with a rule for finding the next one. This could be something like "add two each time" or "multiply the previous number by two." There are many special sequences that are important in maths, like the square number sequence {0, 1, 4, 9, 16, 25, 36, 49, …} and the cube number sequence {1, 8, 27, 64, 125, 216, 343, 512, …}

The Fibonacci Sequence

A sequence that's especially interesting to mathematicians is called the "Fibonacci Sequence," {0, 1, 1, 2, 3, 5, 8, 13, 21, 34, …} The next number is found by adding the two previous ones together. So you add 0 and 1 to get 1, you add 1 and 1 to get 2, you add 1 and 2 to get 3, and so on. It's a sequence that turns up in many unexpected places in real life, and is often found in nature.

> The mathematician Leonardo of Pisa, also known as Fibonacci, posed a problem about the growth of rabbit populations in his 1202 manuscript *Liber Abaci*.

> Fibonacci asked his readers to imagine a population of rabbits. Each pair of rabbits produce a new pair of baby rabbits every month. The rabbits can only produce a new pair when they're more than two months old, and we're assuming that none of them die. If a single pair of rabbits are placed in a field, how many will there be after a year?

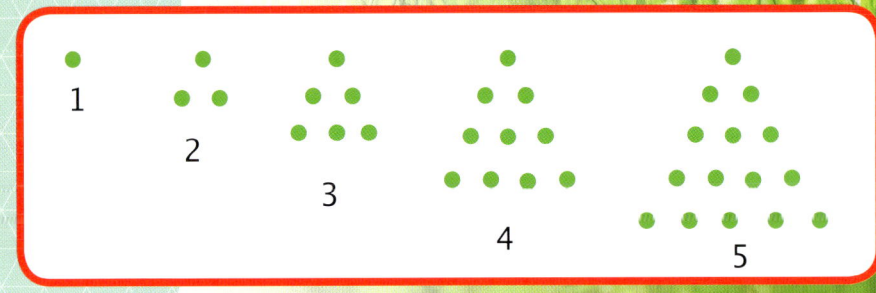

Triangular numbers

Triangular numbers are a sequence made by arranging dots or objects into equilateral triangles, giving 1, 3, 6, 10, 15, 21, 28, 36, 45, …

> If everyone at a party wanted to shake hands once with everyone else at the party, what would be the total number of handshakes? Subtract one from the number of people and look at the triangular number in that position. So if there were five people, look at the fourth triangular number, which has 10 dots. There would be 10 handshakes at the party.

DID YOU KNOW? November 23rd is known as "Fibonacci Day," as it can be written as 11/23.

Count the number of petals on a flower, or look at a pineapple or the head of a sunflower. You'll encounter numbers from the Fibonacci sequence over and over again.

At the end of the first month, there is one pair of rabbits. At the end of the second month, there is still only one pair of rabbits, as they aren't old enough to breed yet. At the end of the third month, there are two pairs of rabbits, as the first pair have now had babies.

The sequence goes 1, 1, 2, 3, 5, 8, 13, 21, 34, 55, 89, 144... At the end of the year, there will be 144 pairs of rabbits.

HALL OF FAME: Fibonacci

Leonardo of Pisa, also known as "Fibonacci," was born around 1170 and died around 1250. As well as describing the famous sequence that's named after him, he popularized the Hindu–Arabic numeral system of 0,1,2,3,4... in the West. He met many tradespeople using it as he travelled with his father, and could see how useful the system was.

Weather

Every day, supercomputers process data from weather balloons, satellites, and observing stations. Temperature, air pressure, wind speed, and water levels are run through mathematical models that predict the weather. Forecasts are essential to many people, and maths plays a crucial role in them.

Percentages

Forecasts give the probabilities of certain types of weather. Look at your local forecast and it will give you the chance of rain tomorrow as a percentage. It can help you work out what to wear when you're leaving the house, but if more serious weather like a hurricane is on the way, a forecast could save your life.

Maths is used to predict the course of deadly hurricanes, giving people in their path the chance to escape.

Complex mathematical models use data about current conditions to predict future ones.

MATHS FACT: The Hottest Years on Record

Rank	Year	Rank	Year
1	2016	6	2014
2	2019	7	2010
3	2015	8	2013
4	2017	9	2005
5	2018	10	2009

DID YOU KNOW? The supercomputers used in weather-forecasting have over 10,000 times the processing power of the average personal computer.

Climate modelling is similar to weather forecasting, but it tracks changes over decades rather than hours. Supercomputers that can make trillions of calculations a second are used to model the Earth's climate. They help us understand how the climate has changed over time, what it's likely to be in the future, and how human activity is affecting it.

Weather planes sometimes fly through storms to gather data about them. Other data comes from ships and satellites.

Climate Data

Not all maths to do with climate change is complicated. You can simply look at the data for the hottest years on record and see how many of them have occurred recently.

Attempts to record annual global temperature stretch back to 1850. The ten hottest years since then have all happened in the current century.

Those who live in the path of a storm could be advised to secure their properties and leave the area. If a hurricane is heading for a densely populated area, millions of people could have to evacuate.

Sport

Maths has always been part of sport. All sports have scoring systems, some of which are simple, and some of which are more complicated. Sports fans love to remember statistics about their favourite teams and players. And the people behind sports stars use maths to analyze and improve their performances.

Analysts look at all aspects of an athlete's performance. Shaving just a fraction of a second off their running time could make a big difference.

Small Details

Athletes measure every little detail in pursuit of perfection. Everything from diet to equipment to atmospheric conditions is examined. Slight changes in the shape of cycle helmets or the material used to make swimming costumes could mean the difference between a gold medal and a silver one.

If you hit the treble ring, you multiply the number by three to get your score.

Darts

Some sports and games require mental arithmetic. In darts, you start with 501, and subtract the score of each throw. The object is to get to zero, with the last dart hitting a double.

If you hit the double ring, you multiply the number by two to get your score.

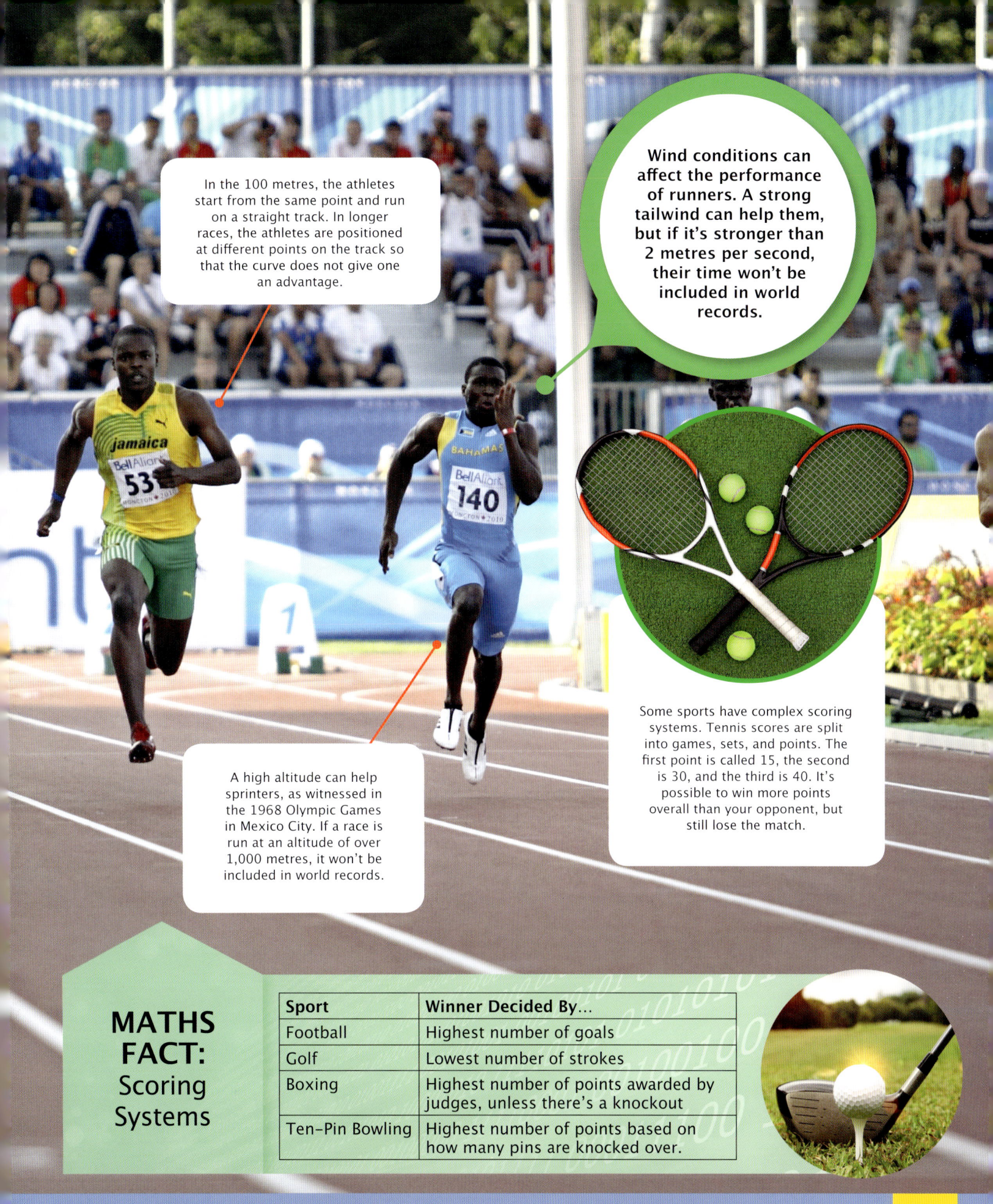

In the 100 metres, the athletes start from the same point and run on a straight track. In longer races, the athletes are positioned at different points on the track so that the curve does not give one an advantage.

Wind conditions can affect the performance of runners. A strong tailwind can help them, but if it's stronger than 2 metres per second, their time won't be included in world records.

A high altitude can help sprinters, as witnessed in the 1968 Olympic Games in Mexico City. If a race is run at an altitude of over 1,000 metres, it won't be included in world records.

Some sports have complex scoring systems. Tennis scores are split into games, sets, and points. The first point is called 15, the second is 30, and the third is 40. It's possible to win more points overall than your opponent, but still lose the match.

MATHS FACT: Scoring Systems

Sport	Winner Decided By...
Football	Highest number of goals
Golf	Lowest number of strokes
Boxing	Highest number of points awarded by judges, unless there's a knockout
Ten-Pin Bowling	Highest number of points based on how many pins are knocked over.

DID YOU KNOW? The time it takes a runner to respond to a starting signal is known as their "reaction time." A reaction time of less than 0.1 seconds counts as a false start.

Logic

You've probably been told at some point that something isn't logical. But what does "logic" mean, and why is it part of maths? Like so many things, our ideas about logic can be traced back to ancient Greece, where the philosopher Aristotle developed formal ways of expressing and judging arguments.

Algebra

Logic became an important part of maths in the 19th century, when British mathematician George Boole applied the methods of algebra to logic. Mathematical arguments could be written in strict forms that made it easy to judge if they were valid. Decades after Boole's death, his work had a massive influence on the development of computer circuits.

Artificial intelligence (AI) is the simulation of intelligence in robots and machines.

Logic provides models of rational thinking that can be used in machines. AI aims to create machines that can choose actions with the best chance of achieving a certain goal.

HALL OF FAME: Aristotle

Aristotle was a Greek philosopher who was born in 384 BCE and died in 322 BCE, and is one of the most important figures in history. In addition to his work on logic, Aristotle pioneered subjects such as biology, botany, chemistry, physics, politics, poetry, ethics, and zoology. His ideas have had a huge influence for centuries, and we continue to debate them today.

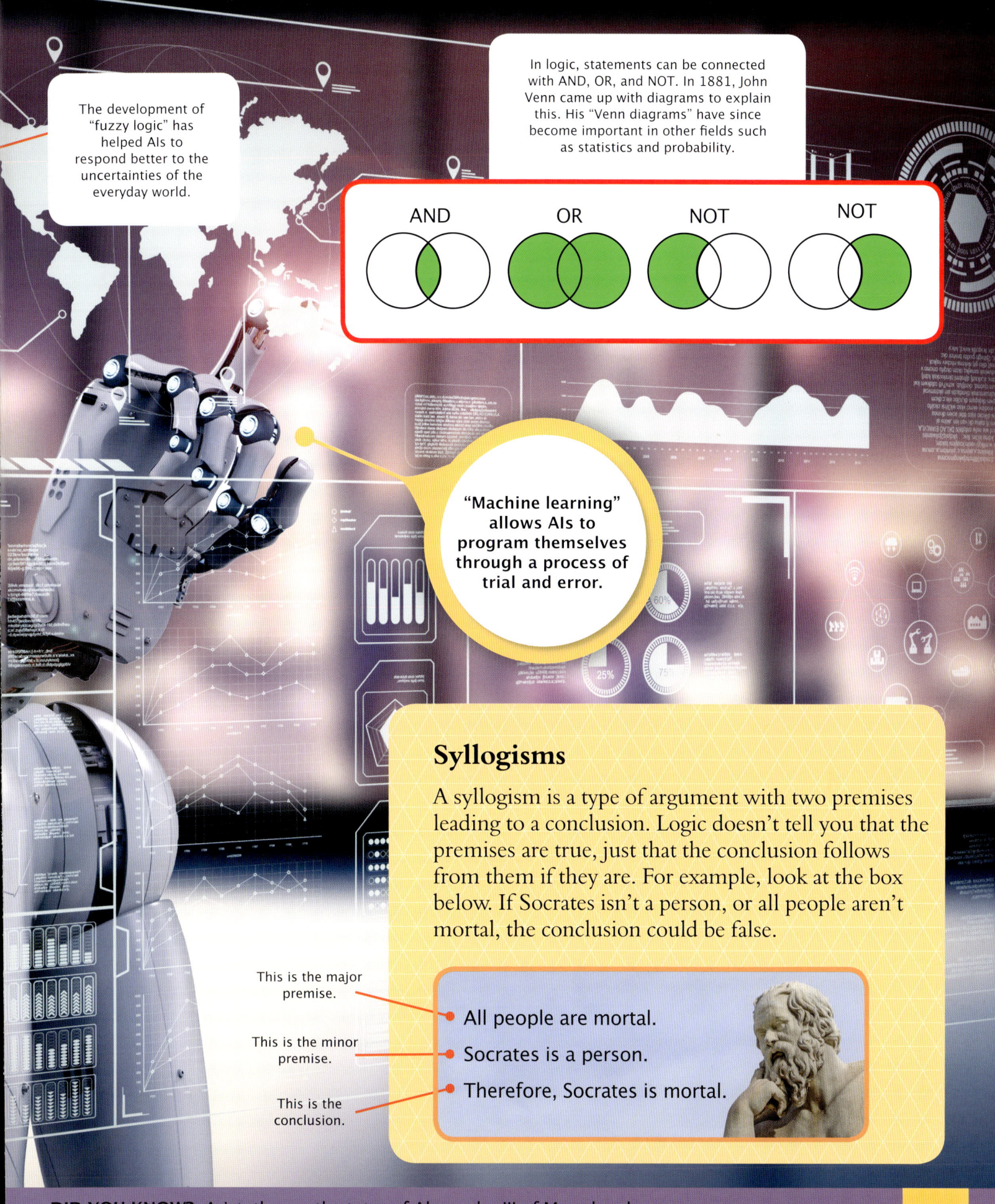

The development of "fuzzy logic" has helped AIs to respond better to the uncertainties of the everyday world.

In logic, statements can be connected with AND, OR, and NOT. In 1881, John Venn came up with diagrams to explain this. His "Venn diagrams" have since become important in other fields such as statistics and probability.

AND　　OR　　NOT　　NOT

"Machine learning" allows AIs to program themselves through a process of trial and error.

Syllogisms

A syllogism is a type of argument with two premises leading to a conclusion. Logic doesn't tell you that the premises are true, just that the conclusion follows from them if they are. For example, look at the box below. If Socrates isn't a person, or all people aren't mortal, the conclusion could be false.

This is the major premise.
This is the minor premise.
This is the conclusion.

- All people are mortal.
- Socrates is a person.
- Therefore, Socrates is mortal.

DID YOU KNOW? Aristotle was the tutor of Alexander III of Macedon, known as "Alexander the Great."

Glossary

ALGEBRA A branch of maths that uses letters to stand in for unknown numbers.

AREA The space inside a two-dimensional object.

BASE The amount of digits in a number system. For example, base 2 uses the digits 0 and 1, and base 10 uses 0, 1, 2, 3, 4, 5, 6, 7, 8, and 9. "Base" also refers to the number that gets multiplied when using a power. For example, in 2^3, the base is 2.

BINARY The base 2 number system, which uses only the digits 0 and 1.

BIT The smallest unit of data in computing. It's a single binary digit, which can be 0 or 1.

BYTE A unit of data used in computing, equivalent to eight bits. For example, 10010101.

CELSIUS A temperature scale that uses the freezing point of water as zero degrees.

CIRCUMFERENCE The distance around a circle.

CODE A system of numbers, letters, or symbols used to represent others so information can be kept secret.

COMPUTER A machine that can store and process data. In the past, the term referred to people who made calculations too.

CO-ORDINATES A set of values that describe the position of something on a grid or map.

CORRELATION A link between two sets of data, which can be either positive or negative.

DATA The numbers, measurements, and observations that are gathered and analyzed in statistics.

DECIMAL Relating to the number 10. It can refer to the base 10 number system, which features the digits 0, 1, 2, 3, 4, 5, 6, 7, 8, and 9. A "decimal" can also mean a number that features a decimal point followed by digits showing a value smaller than one, such as 4.2.

DENOMINATOR The number on the bottom of a fraction, which shows how many equal parts the whole has been divided into.

DIAMETER The distance across the middle of a circle. It is twice the length of the radius.

DIMENSION A measurement of length in a direction. A line has one dimension, a square has two dimensions, and a cube has three dimensions.

DIGIT A single symbol used to write a number. We use the digits 0, 1, 2, 3, 4, 5, 6, 7, 8, and 9 in the base 10 system.

ENCRYPTION Converting information into a code to keep it secret.

EQUATION A statement that two things are equal, such as 2 + 2 = 4.

ESTIMATE A value which might not be the exact right answer, but is close enough to be useful.

EXPONENTIAL GROWTH When something is growing in relation to its current value, such as always doubling.

FAHRENHEIT A temperature scale that sets zero at 32 degrees below the freezing point of water.

FRACTION A part of a whole amount, such as $1/2$.

FREQUENCY How often something happens. In statistics, it refers to the number of times a value occurs in a data set.

GEOMETRY The mathematical study of shapes, size, and space. "Plane geometry" deals with flat shapes such as lines, squares and circles, while "solid geometry" deals with three-dimensional shapes such as spheres, cubes, and pyramids.

GIGABYTE A unit of data used in computing, equal to around one billion bytes.

IRRATIONAL NUMBER A number that can't be written as a simple fraction, such as e or pi.

KELVIN A temperature scale that starts at absolute zero, the lowest possible temperature.

LINEAR GROWTH When something is growing by the same amount each time.

MEAN The value found by adding all the numbers in a data set together, and diving the sum by the number of values.

126

MEDIAN The middle value of a data set, if all the values are listed in order from lowest to highest.

MEGABYTE A unit of data used in computing, equal to around one million bytes.

MODE The value that appears most often in a data set.

NEGATIVE NUMBERS Numbers that are less than zero, written with a minus sign before them, such as -3.

NUMERATOR The top number of a fraction, which shows how many parts of the whole you have.

OPERATION A mathematical process such as addition, subtraction, multiplication, division, or squaring.

PERCENTAGE The part of a whole expressed in hundredths. For example, if you have 5% of something, it means you have five hundredths of it.

PERIMETER The distance around the edge of a two-dimensional shape.

PI The ratio of a circle's circumference to its diameter. Measure the distance around a circle and divide it by the distance across it, and you'll get pi, which is 3.14 to two decimal places.

POLYGON A two-dimensional shape with straight sides, such as a triangle, rectangle, and pentagon. A regular polygon has equal sides and angles.

POLYHEDRON A solid shape with flat surfaces, such as a pyramid or cube. Spheres and cones are not polyhedrons, as they have curved surfaces.

POSITIVE NUMBERS Numbers that are greater than zero.

POWER A small number placed at the top right of another that tells you how many times to multiply the number by itself. For example, 2^3 means $2 \times 2 \times 2$, which is 8.

PRIME NUMBERS Numbers that can only be exactly divided by themselves and 1.

PROBABILITY The chance that a particular event will occur.

RADIUS The distance from the centre of a circle to its circumference. It is half the length of the diameter.

RATIO A comparison between two values that shows their sizes in relation to each other, written in form such as "3:1" or "3 to 1."

REFLECTIONAL SYMMETRY A type of symmetry in which half a shape is a reflection of the other half.

ROTATIONAL SYMMETRY A type of symmetry in which a shape can be turned around a fixed point and still look the same.

SAMPLE A small group taken from a larger group. Studying a sample can help you learn about the whole group.

SEQUENCE A list of numbers in order that are generated according to a certain rule.

STATISTICS The branch of mathematics that deals with the collection and interpretation of data.

TALLYING Making marks to keep count. The marks are often grouped into fives.

THEOREM A mathematical statement that can be proved to be true.

TEMPERATURE A measure of how hot or cold something is.

TERABYTE A unit of data used in computing, equal to around one trillion bytes.

TESSELATING A flat surface which is covered with a geometric shape, with no overlaps and no gaps.

VOLUME The space inside a three-dimensional object.

WHOLE NUMBER The term used to refer to the numbers 0, 1, 2, 3, and so on. Whole numbers don't include fractions or negative numbers.

Index

abacus 4-5, 86-87
absolute zero 11
addition 6-7, 86, 100
algebra 22-23, 106, 124
algorithms 100-101
arches 98
architecture 24, 28, 98-99, 115
area 27, 33, 34-35, 36, 45, 76, 83, 105
athletics 56, 122-123

Babylonians 23, 36, 48, 100
bar charts 76
barcodes 90-91
base 2 12-13
base 8 13
base 10 12-13, 48
base 12 12, 48
base 16 13
base 60 13, 48
bases and powers 12-13
Bayes' theorem 110-111
Benford's Law 72-73
binary 12-13, 86
bytes 17

Caesar cipher 93
calendars 50-51
Celsius 10-11, 52
chaos theory 84-85
China 8, 11, 50-51, 86, 106
cholera 117
circles 27, 30-31, 36-37, 38, 40, 45, 63, 77
circumference 36-37
climate change 75, 120-121
clocks 7, 9, 13, 28, 48-49
co-ordinates 64-65
codes 90-94
computer-aided design 98
computers 12, 17, 19, 21, 24, 42-43, 85, 86, 88-89, 92, 98, 100-101, 103, 104, 109, 113, 114, 120-121, 124
correlation 70-71
counting 6-8, 11, 58, 88
COVID-19 116-117
Cranmer abacus 87
cube numbers 14-15, 118
Cuneiform 6

dance 106
darts 39, 122
decimals 18, 23, 36, 57, 82-83, 85
degrees 28, 64
density 53-55
diameter 16, 36-37
division 7, 12, 20, 22, 36, 48, 50, 68-69, 80, 83

Egypt 5, 36, 48
elections 73
encryption 92, 94-95
Enigma machine 92
Eulerian paths 104
exponential growth 78-79, 117

Fahrenheit 11, 52
Fibonacci sequence 118-119
fractals 42-44, 114
fractions 22-23, 36
frequency 72-73

game theory 112-113
geodesic domes 5, 98-99
golden ratio 45
gravity 54-55, 84, 102
Greeks 5, 20, 26, 28-29, 30, 32, 37, 52, 108, 124
Gregorian calendar 50-51

hacking 94
hexagons 30-31, 44
Hindu-Arabic numerals 7, 119

infinity 18-19, 38-39
inflation 58
irrational numbers 36, 105

Julian calendar 50

Kelvin 11, 56
Klein bottle 41
Kryptos 92

leap years 50-51
light years 16-17, 62-63
line graphs 74-76, 79
linear growth 78-79
logic 124-125

maps 12, 64-65, 110-111, 117
metric system 46, 57
microchips 88
Mobius strips 40-41
money 9, 11, 58-59, 79, 82, 89, 94, 110, 112
months 50-51, 74-75, 118-119
moon 50-51, 54-55, 62, 102-103
multiplication 6-7, 11, 14-15, 20-21, 23, 32, 36-37, 51, 63, 83, 118, 122
music 66, 108-109

negative numbers 10-11, 16
negative correlation 71
nodes and edges 104

outliers 68

pandemics 116-117
passwords 94-95
patterns 20, 30-31, 36, 42-45, 66, 72-75, 84-85, 90, 98
pay-off matrix 113
pedestrian crossings 97
pentagons 30-31, 38, 99
percentages 23, 58-59, 67, 73, 120
perspective 114-115
phishing 94
phones 12, 68, 91, 103, 104
pi 36-37
pie charts 77
polygons 30-31, 37, 45
polyhedrons 32-34
predictions 52-53, 66, 73, 74, 84-85, 110-111, 120-121

prime numbers 20-21
probability 19, 73, 80-81, 110-111, 120

QR codes 91

ratios 34, 45, 54, 64-65,
Roman numerals 7, 8
rounding 82-83, 85

sampling 66-67, 69, 82-83
satellites 53, 102, 120-121
scatter graphs 70
sequences 42, 79, 88-89, 100, 118-119
SI units 56-57
Sierpinski triangle 43
social networks 105
solar system 61-63
solar years 50-51
soroban 86-87
space travel 4, 55, 62-63, 102-103
spam filters 111
spheres 32-34, 40, 114
square numbers 14-15, 118
square roots 14-15
squares 27, 30-31, 38, 40, 45, 91, 106, 114
suan pan 86-87
subtraction 6-7, 10, 86, 122
sudoku 106-107
Sumerians 6, 48
syllogisms 125
symmetry 38-39, 44, 98, 109

tallying 6
temperature 10-11, 52-53, 56, 74-75, 120-121
tessellation 31, 44-45, 98, 115
time signatures 109
tennis 123
topology 40-41, 113
traffic 60-61, 96-97
triangles 26-27, 98-99, 114, 118

vanishing point 115
velocity 60-61
Venn diagrams 77, 125
volume 32-35, 54

wind chill 53

zero 8-11, 15-17, 61, 122